budgetbooks

CLASSIC ROCK

T0039578

ISBN 978-1-4768-9952-7

HAL•LEONARD®
CORPORATION

7777 W. BLUEMOUND RD. P.O. BOX 13819 MILWAUKEE, WI 53213

Visit Hal Leonard Online at
www.halleonard.com

CONTENTS

ADDICTED TO LOVE

Words and Music by
ROBERT PALMER

The lights are on, but you're not
signs, but you can't
Instrumental

home: your   mind _   is not your   own.   Your heart
read: you're run-ning at ____   a dif-f'rent speed.   Your heart

C7 ... **G7**

sweats,   your bod-y shakes;   an-oth-er   kiss   is what it
beats   in dou-ble time,   an-oth-er   kiss   and you'll be

End instrumental

takes.   You can't   sleep,   you can't   eat;   there's no
mine.   A one-track mind;   you can't be saved;   ob-liv-i-
The lights are   on,   but you're not home;   your

F7 ... **C7**

doubt _   you're in   deep.   Your throat is tight,   you can't
on ____   is all you crave.   If   there's _ some   left for
will ____ is not your own.   Your heart _ sweats,   your teeth

6

8

AFTER MIDNIGHT

Words and Music by
J.J. CALE

Moderate Rock beat, in 2

Af - ter mid - night, __ we're gon - na let it all __ hang down.
Af - ter mid - night, __ we're gon - na shake your tam - bou - rine.

Af - ter mid - night, __ we're gon - na chug - a - lug __ and
Af - ter mid - night, __ it's all gon - na be peach - es __ and

shout. _____
cream. _____

We're gon-na
We're gon-na

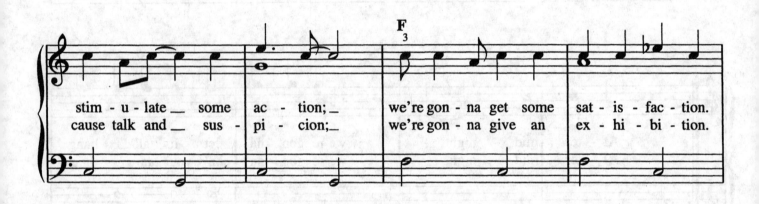

stim - u - late __ some ac - tion; __ we're gon - na get some sat - is - fac - tion.
cause talk and __ sus - pi - cion; __ we're gon - na give an ex - hi - bi - tion.

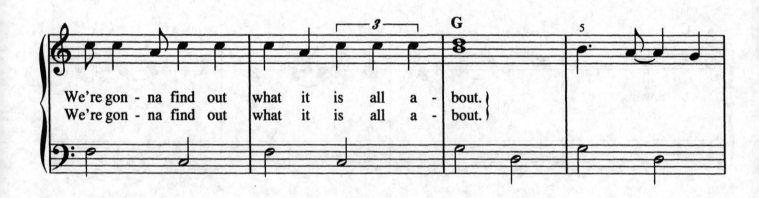

We're gon - na find out what it is all a - bout.
We're gon - na find out what it is all a - bout.

Af - ter mid - night, __

we're gon - na let it all __ hang down.

Af - ter mid - night, __

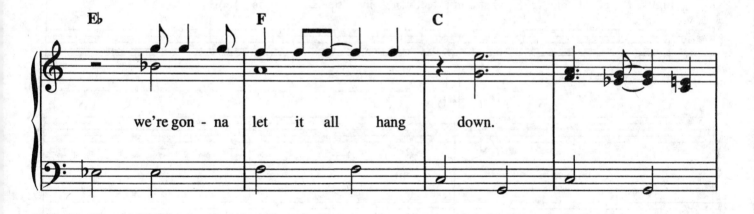

we're gon - na let it all hang down.

AMANDA

Words and Music by
TOM SCHOLZ

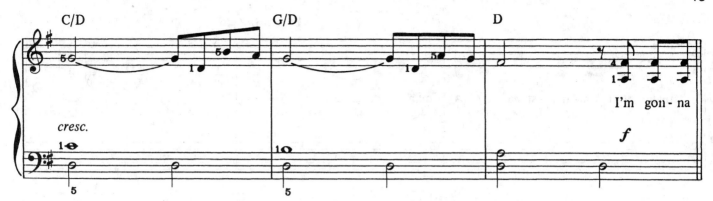

C/D   G/D   D

I'm gon - na

cresc.   *f*

Chorus

Em   Am7   D

take you by sur - prise and make you re - al - ize, A - man - da.

mp

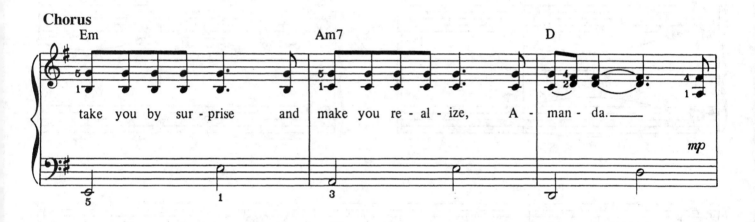

Em   Am7

I'm gon - na tell you right a - way; I can't wait an - oth - er day, A-

f

D   Em

man - da. I'm gon - na say it like a man and

mp   *f*

I swear it's not a lie, ___ girl. ___ To-mor-row may be too late. ___

___

You, you and I, ___ girl, we can

share a life ___ to-geth-er. It's now or nev-er, and to-

mor-row may be too late. ___ Oh. ___

And

feel - in' the way___ I do,___ I don't wan - na wait my whole life

through_____ to say

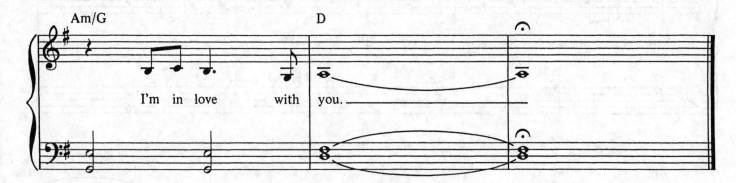

I'm in love with you._____

Additional Lyrics

2. And I, I'm gettin' too close again.
   I don't wanna see it end.
   If I tell you tonight, will you turn out the light
   And walk away knowin' I love you?
   Chorus

3. And I feel like today's the day.
   I'm lookin' for the words to say.
   Do you wanna be free? Are you ready for me
   To feel this way? I don't wanna lose ya.

4. So, it may be too soon, I know.
   The feelin' takes so long to grow.
   If I tell you today, will you turn me away
   And let me go? I don't wanna lose you.
   Chorus

BABY HOLD ON

Words and Music by EDDIE MONEY
and JAMES DOUGLAS LYON

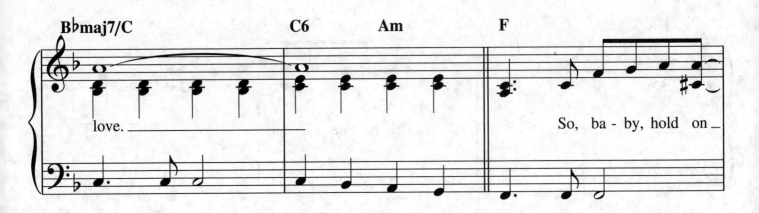

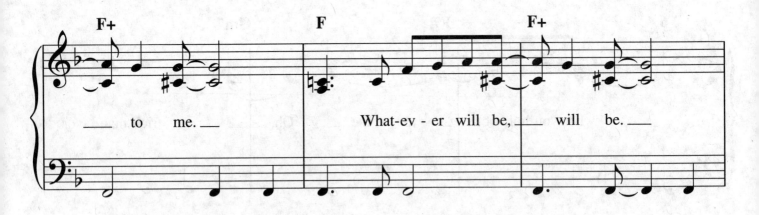

AQUALUNG

Words and Music by IAN ANDERSON
and JENNIE ANDERSON

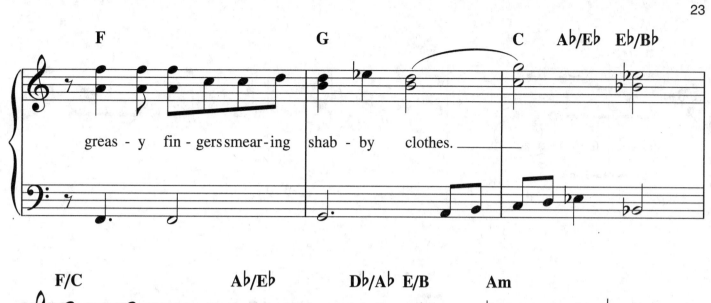

greas - y fin - gers smear-ing shab - by clothes. _____

Hey, Aq - ua- lung.

Dry-ing in the cold sun,

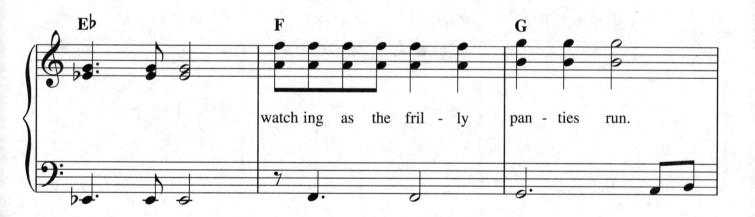

watch ing as the fril - ly pan - ties run.

Hey, Aq - ua- lung.

Faster

f Do you still re - mem - ber De -

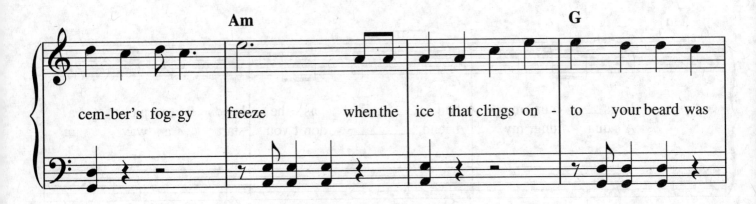

cem-ber's fog-gy freeze when the ice that clings on - to your beard was

scream - ing ag - o - ny? And you snatch your rat - tling

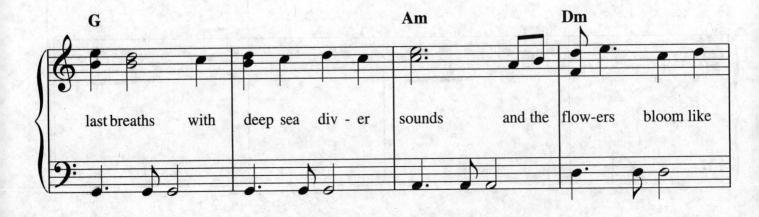

last breaths with deep sea div - er sounds and the flow-ers bloom like

BANG THE DRUM ALL DAY

Words and Music by
TODD RUNDGREN

BETH

Words and Music by BOB EZRIN,
STANLEY PENRIDGE and PETER CRISS

Rock Ballad, with feeling

Beth, I hear you call-in', but I can't come home right now.
You say you feel so emp-ty, that our house just ain't a home.

Me and the boys are play - in' and we just can't find the sound.
I'm al-ways some - where else and you're al-ways there a - lone.

Just a few more hours, and I'll be right home to you. I

THE BOYS ARE BACK IN TOWN

Words and Music by
PHILIP PARRIS LYNOTT

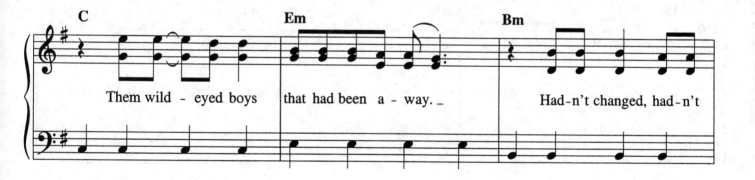

1. Guess who just got back to-day
2.,3. *(See additional lyrics)*

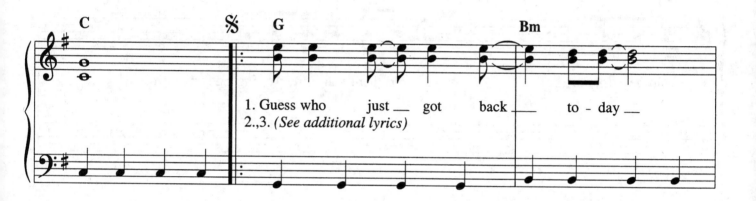

Them wild-eyed boys that had been a-way. Had-n't changed, had-n't

much to say, but, man, I still think them cats are cra-zy.

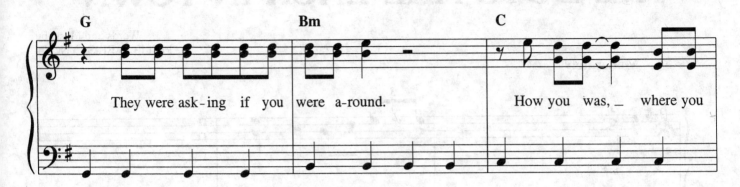

They were ask-ing if you were a-round. How you was, __ where you

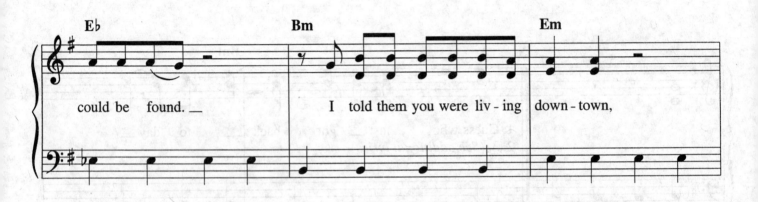

could be found. __ I told them you were liv-ing down-town,

driv-ing all the old men cra-zy. The boys are back in town, the

boys are back in town. I say, the

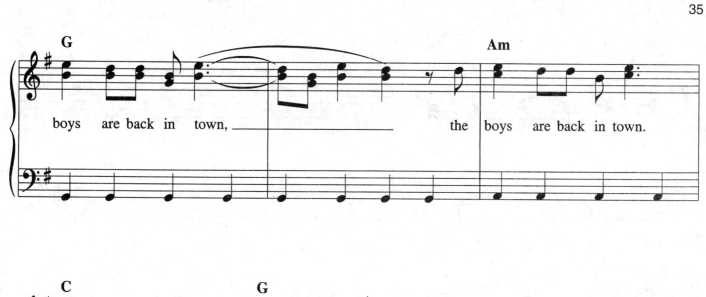

boys are back in town, _____ the boys are back in town.

The boys are back in town, the boys are back in town, the

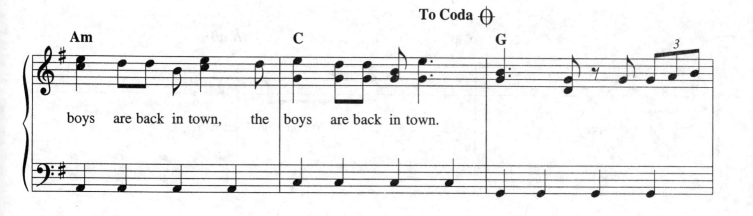

boys are back in town, the boys are back in town.

CODA

Additional Lyrics

2. You know that chick that used to dance a lot?
   Every night she'd be on the floor shaking what she'd got.
   Man, when I tell you she was cool, she was hot.
   I mean she was steaming.

   And that time over at Johnny's place,
   Well, this chick got up and she slapped Johnny's face.
   Man, we just fell about the place.
   If that chick don't wanna know, forget her.

3. Friday night they'll be dressed to kill
   Down at Dino's Bar and Grill.
   The drink will flow and the blood will spill,
   And if the boys want to fight, you better let 'em.

   That jukebox in the corner blasting out my favorite song.
   The nights are getting warmer, it won't be long.
   It won't be long 'til summer comes,
   Now that the boys are here again.

BREAKDOWN

Words and Music by
TOM PETTY

BURNING DOWN THE HOUSE

Words by DAVID BYRNE
Music by DAVID BYRNE, CHRIS FRANTZ,
JERRY HARRISON and TINA WEYMOUTH

43

CHANGES

Words and Music by
DAVID BOWIE

Still don't know what I was look-ing for __ and my time was run-ning
I watch the rip - ples change their size __ but nev - er leave the

wild; a mil - lion dead-end __ streets.
stream of warm im - per - ma - nence. And

Ev - 'ry time I thought I'd
so the days flow

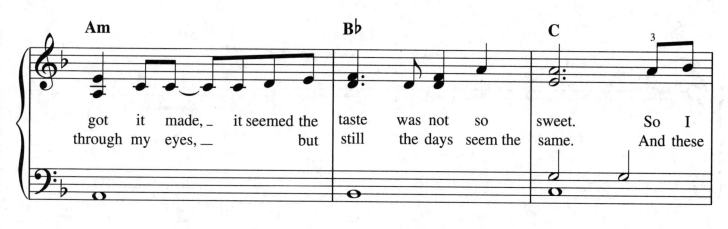

got it made, _ it seemed the taste was not so sweet. So I
through my eyes, _ but still the days seem the same. And these

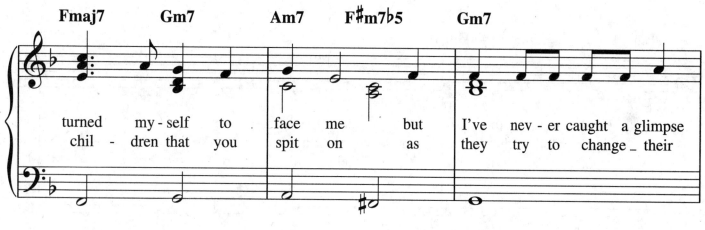

turned my - self to face me but I've nev - er caught a glimpse
chil - dren that you spit on as they try to change _ their

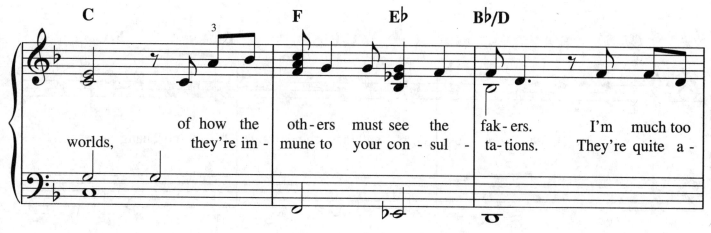

worlds, of how the oth - ers must see the fak - ers. I'm much too
they're im - mune to your con - sul - ta - tions. They're quite a -

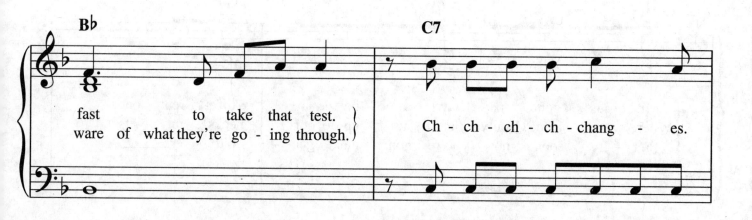

fast to take that test.
ware of what they're go - ing through.

Ch - ch - ch - ch - chang - es.

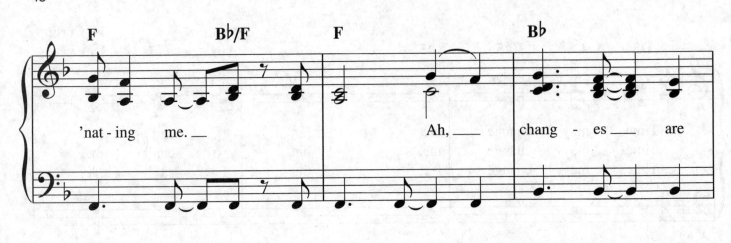

'nat - ing me. ___   Ah, ___ chang - es ___ are

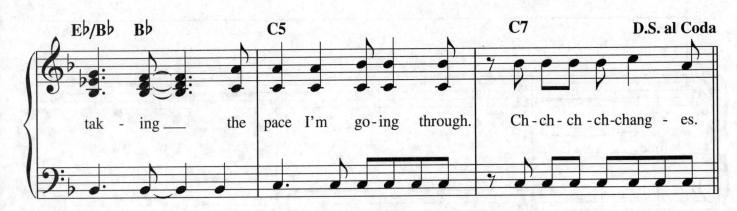

tak - ing ___ the pace I'm go-ing through.   Ch - ch - ch - ch-chang - es.

CODA

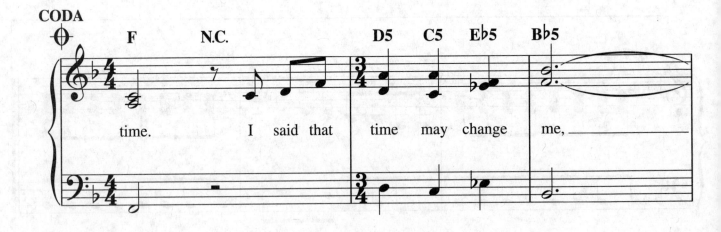

time.   I said that   time   may change   me, _____

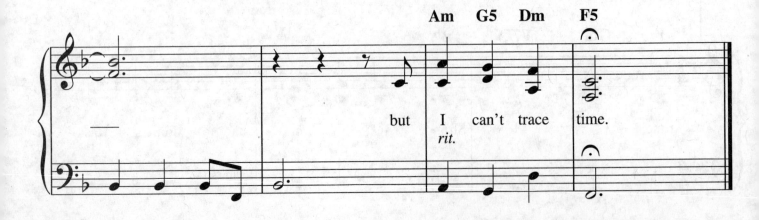

___   but   I   can't trace   time.
rit.

CHINA GROVE

Words and Music by
TOM JOHNSTON

COME SAIL AWAY

Words and Music by
DENNIS DeYOUNG

DAY TRIPPER

Words and Music by JOHN LENNON
and PAUL McCARTNEY

DEACON BLUES

Words and Music by WALTER BECKER
and DONALD FAGEN

This is the day of the ex-
My back to the wall, a vic-tim of

pand - ing man.
laugh - ing chance.

sax - o - phone.___   I'll play   just___   what I   feel.___

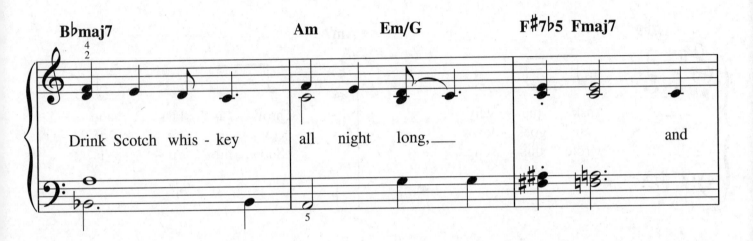

Drink Scotch whis - key   all   night   long,___   and

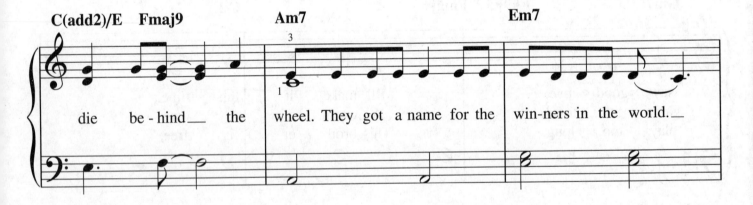

die   be - hind___   the   wheel. They got a name for the   win - ners in the world.___

I want a   name___   when I lose.___   They call Al - a - bam - a the

DEAR MR. FANTASY

Words and Music by JAMES CAPALDI,
CHRIS WOOD and STEVE WINWOOD

Dear Mis-ter Fan - ta-sy, play us a tune, ___ some-thing to make us all hap- py. ___ Do an - y - thing, _ take us out of this gloom. ___ Sing a song, play gui-tar, make it snap-py. ___

DOMINO

Words and Music by
VAN MORRISON

Moderately fast

Don't wan-na dis-cuss __ it. ___
There's no need for ar - gu - ment; ___

Think it's time __ for a change. __
there's no ar - gu-ment at all. __

You may get dis-
And if you nev-

gust - ed, ___
er hear from him,

start think - ing that I'm strange. _
that just mean she did - n't call.

DON'T FEAR THE REAPER

Words and Music by
DONALD ROESER

THE FIRST CUT IS THE DEEPEST

Words and Music by
CAT STEVENS

I would have giv-en you all of my heart, but there's some-one who's torn it a-part. And she's

want you by my side, just to help me dry the tears that I've cried. And I'm

DREAM ON

Words and Music by
STEVEN TYLER

Moderately slow

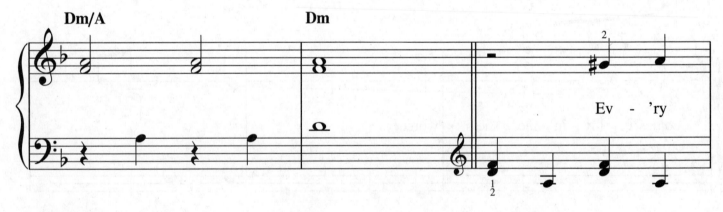

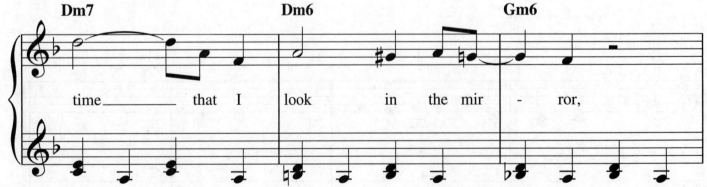

I know it's ev-'ry-bod-y's sin; you got to lose to know

how to win.

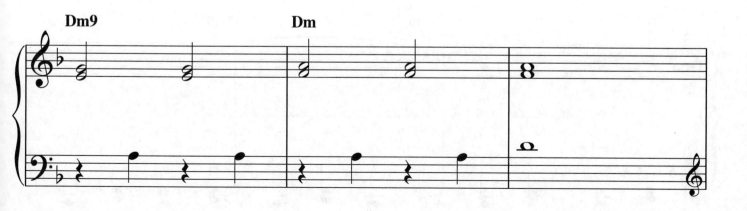

DREAM WEAVER

Words and Music by
GARY WRIGHT

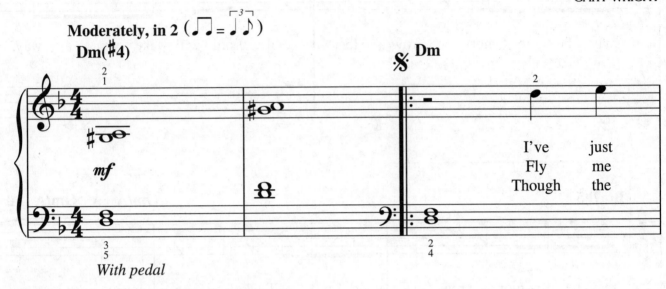

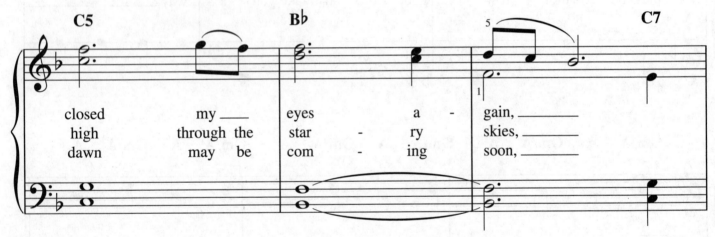

FOR WHAT IT'S WORTH

Words and Music by
STEPHEN STILLS

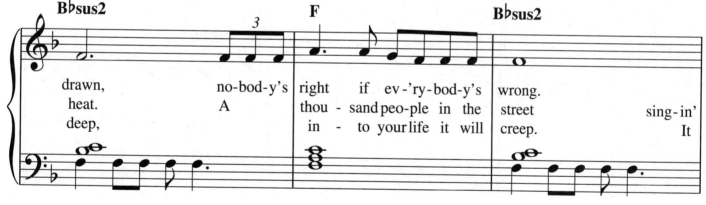

from   be - hind. I think it's time   we   stop,   chil - dren, what's that   sound? _
our   side."   Stop,   chil - dren, what's that   sound? _

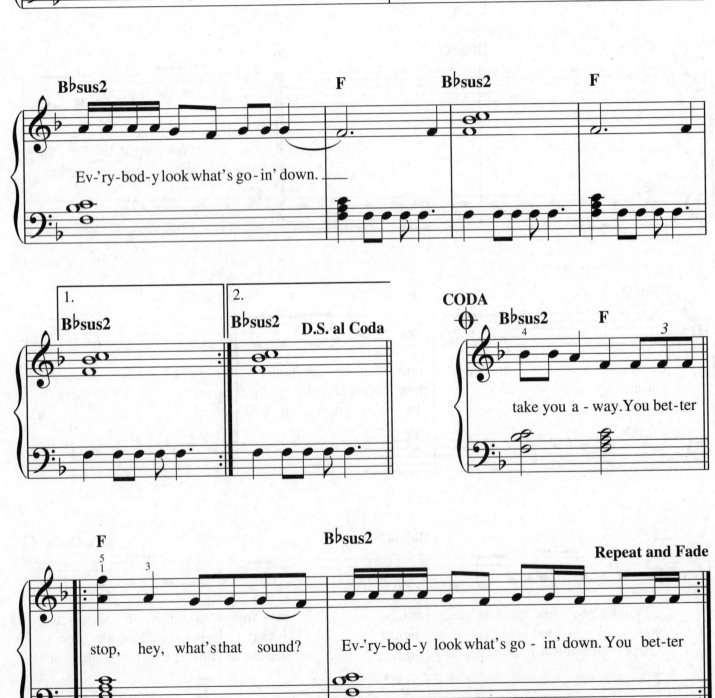

Ev-'ry-bod-y look what's go - in' down.

1. 2. **D.S. al Coda**

CODA

take you a - way. You bet-ter

stop,   hey,   what's that   sound?

Repeat and Fade

Ev-'ry-bod-y look what's go - in' down. You bet-ter

FROM THE BEGINNING

Words and Music by
GREG LAKE

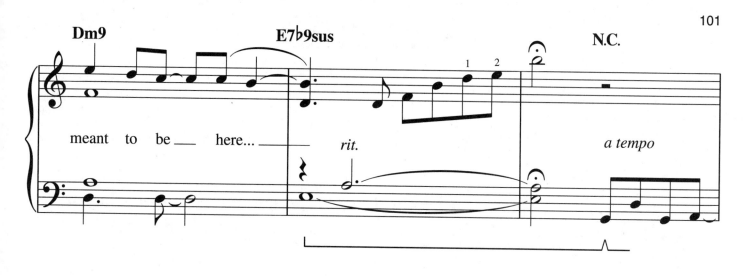

meant to be ___ here... _____ *rit.* _____ *a tempo*

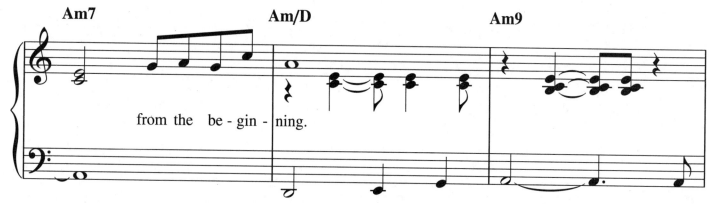

from the be - gin - ning.

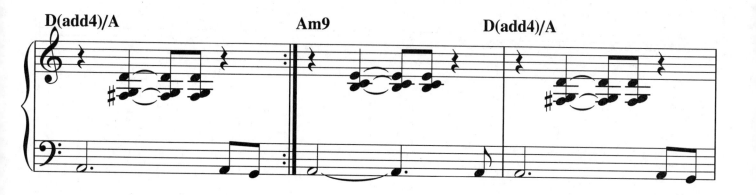

rit. ___ *p*

FREE BIRD

Words and Music by ALLEN COLLINS
and RONNIE VAN ZANT

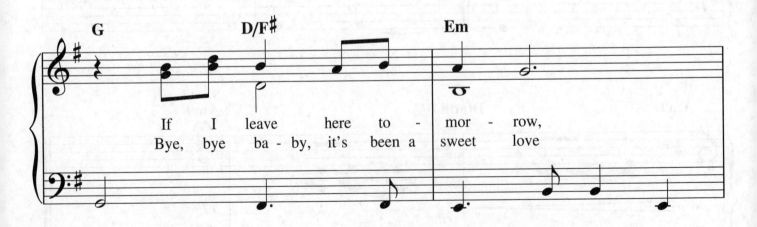

If I leave here to - mor - row,
Bye, bye ba - by, it's been a sweet love

GLORIA

Words and Music by
VAN MORRISON

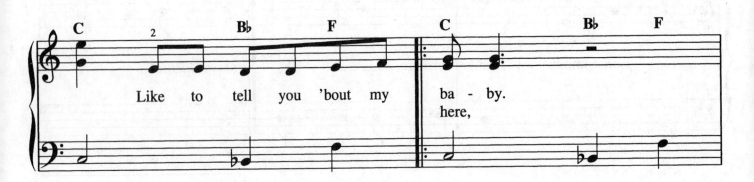

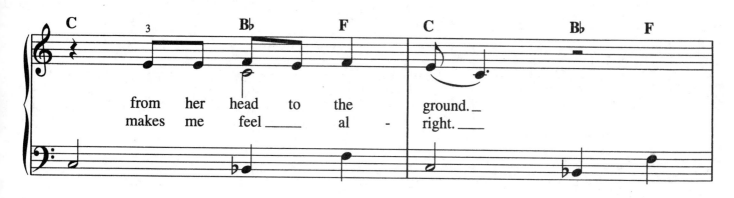

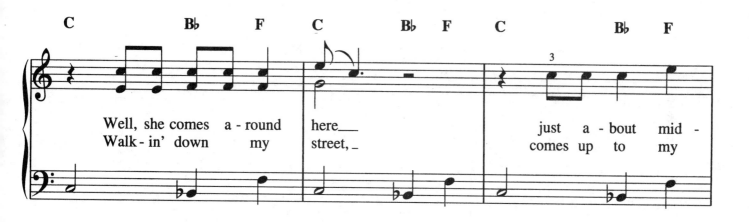

108

GO YOUR OWN WAY

Words and Music by
LINDSEY BUCKINGHAM

give you___ my world.
give you___ the world.

How___ can I___
O - pen up.___

___ when___ you won't take it from___ me?
___ Ev - 'ry-thing's wait - ing for___ you.

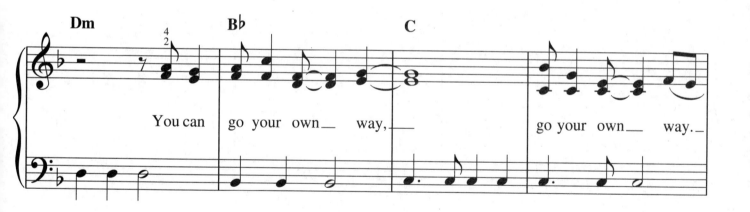

You can go your own___ way,___ go your own___ way.___

___ You can call it an - oth - er lone - ly day.___

You can go___ your own___ way,___ go your own___ way.

You can go your own___ way,___

go your own___ way.___ You can call it an - oth -

- er lone - ly day.___

HIGHER LOVE

Words and Music by WILL JENNINGS
and STEVE WINWOOD

A HARD DAY'S NIGHT

Words and Music by JOHN LENNON
and PAUL McCARTNEY

I LOVE ROCK 'N ROLL

Words and Music by ALAN MERRILL
and JAKE HOOKER

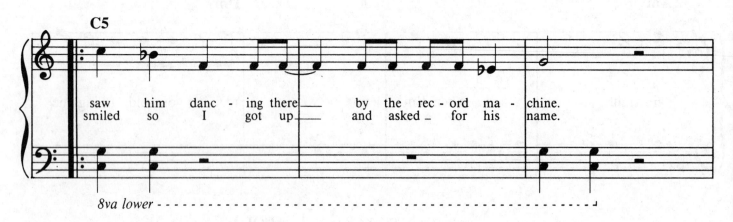

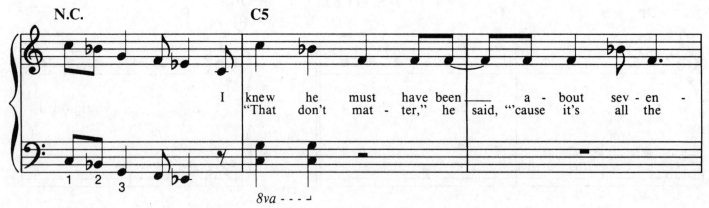

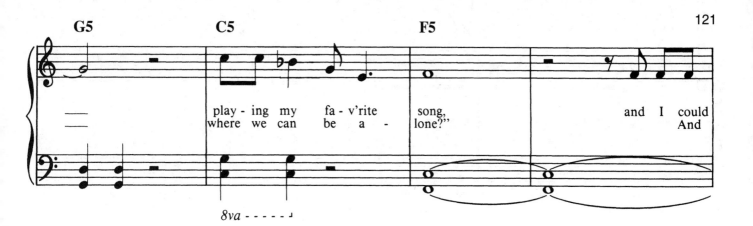

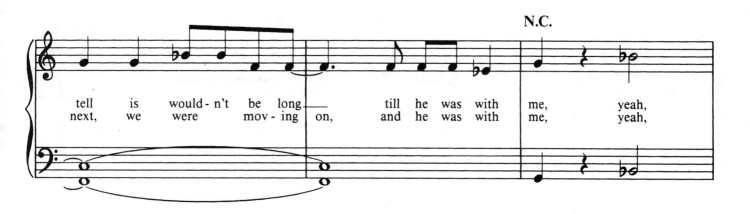

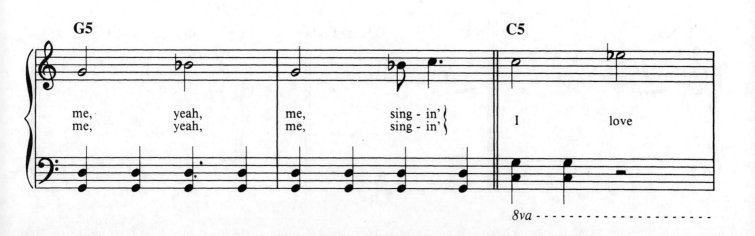

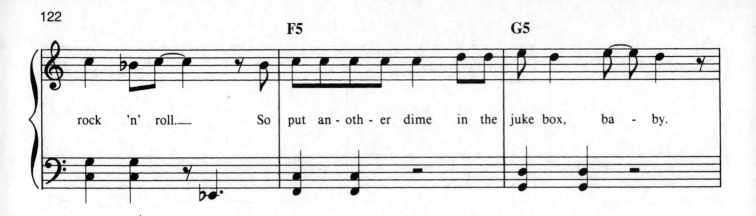

rock 'n' roll.___ So put an-oth-er dime in the juke box, ba - by.

I love rock 'n' roll.___ So come and take your time and

dance with me.

8va lower

1. N.C. He

2. N.C. D.S. al Coda I

CODA G5 C5

dance with me.

8va

IN THE AIR TONIGHT

Words and Music by
PHIL COLLINS

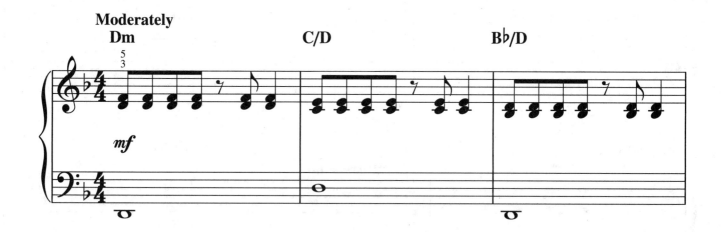

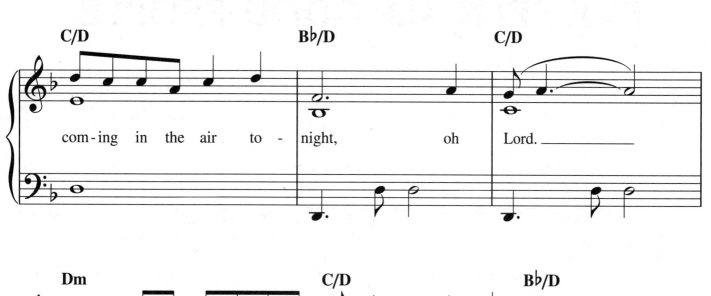

com-ing in the air to - night, oh Lord.

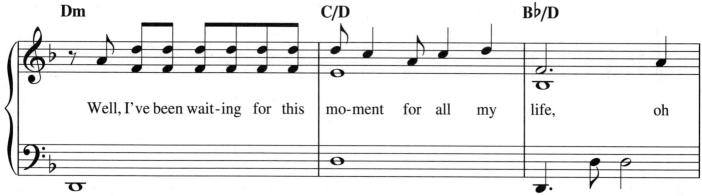

Well, I've been wait-ing for this mo-ment for all my life, oh

Lord.

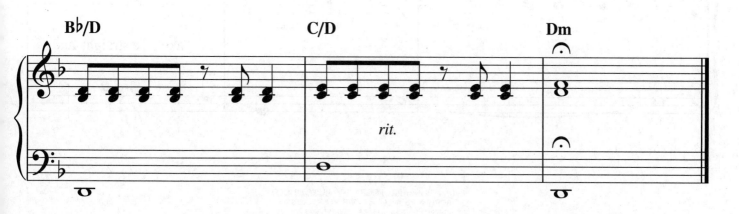

rit.

I'VE SEEN ALL GOOD PEOPLE

Words and Music by JON ANDERSON
and CHRIS SQUIRE

Moderately

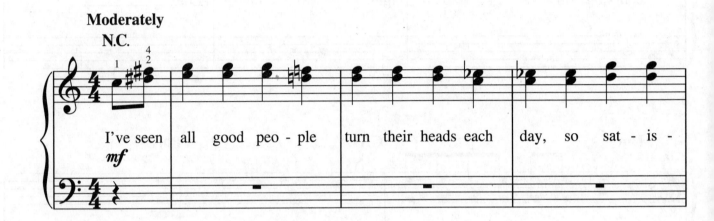

I've seen all good peo-ple turn their heads each day, so sat-is-

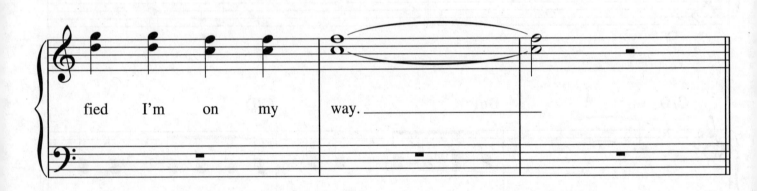

fied I'm on my way.

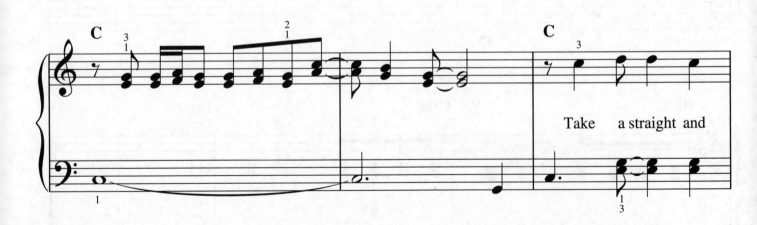

Take a straight and

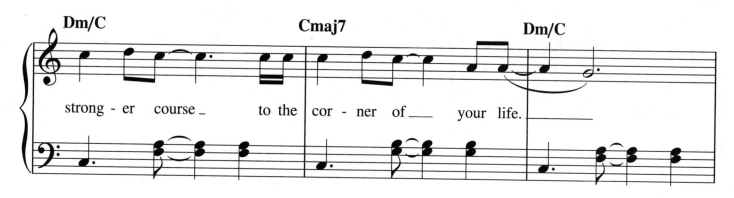

strong - er course _ to the cor - ner of __ your life. __

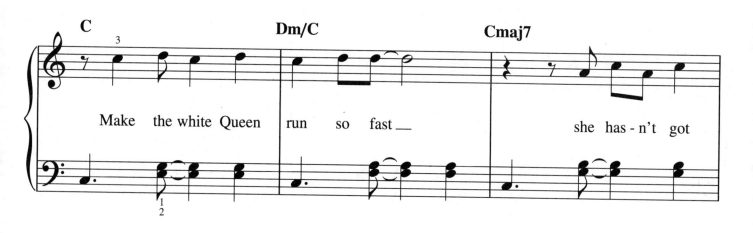

Make the white Queen run so fast __ she has - n't got

time _____ to make you __ wise. _____

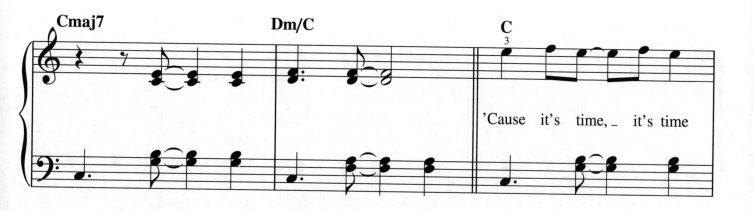

'Cause it's time, _ it's time

Dm/C   **Cmaj7**   **Dm/C**

in time   with your   time   and ___   its news   is   cap - tured _____

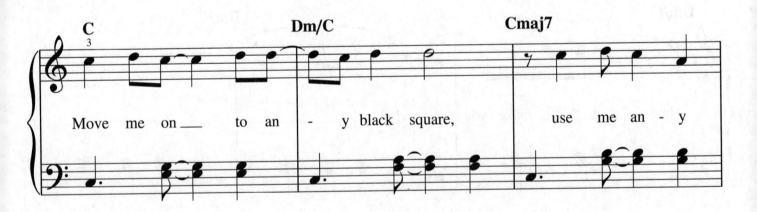

for ___   the   Queen   to   use.

C   **Dm/C**   **Cmaj7**

Move   me   on ___   to an - y   black   square,   use   me   an - y

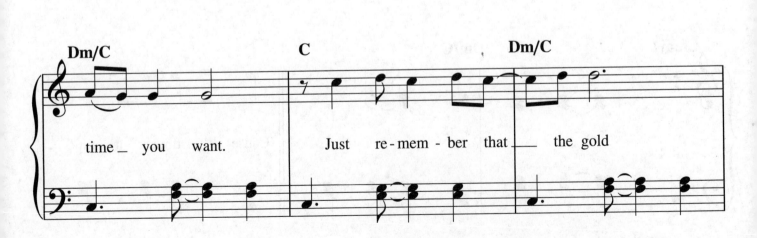

Dm/C   **C**   **Dm/C**

time ___   you   want.   Just   re - mem - ber   that ___   the   gold

Cmaj7

'sfor us all to

Dm/C

cap - ture _____ all we

C

want _____

Dm/C

an - y - where. _

Cmaj7

Yea,

Dm/C

yea, yea, yea. __

C

Don't sur - round your - self _

Dm7

with your - self, _

Cmaj7

move on back two squares. _

Dm

—

C

Send an in - stant com

Dm7

- ment to me. _

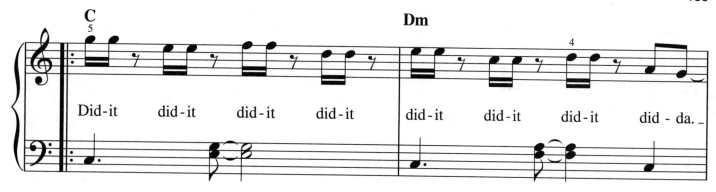

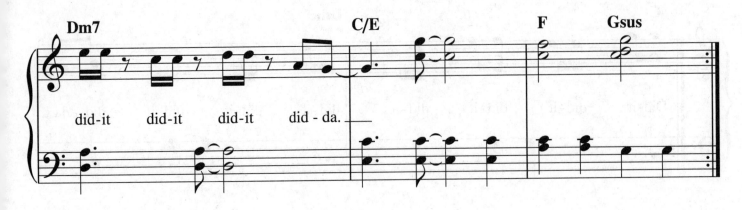

Dm7　　　　　　　　　　　　　　**C/E**　　　　　**F**　　**Gsus**

did-it　　did-it　　did-it　　did - da.

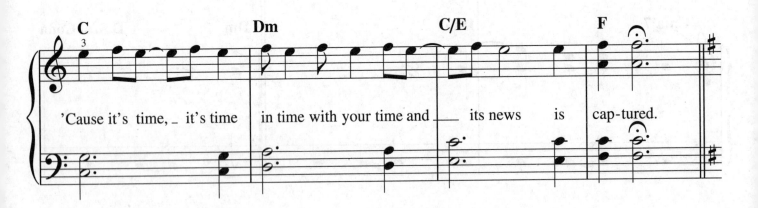

C　　　　　　　　**Dm**　　　　　　　　**C/E**　　　　　**F**

'Cause it's time, _ it's time　in time with your time and _ its news　is　cap-tured.

Moderately bright shuffle

C　　　　　　　　**C7**　　　　　　　　　　**D7**

f

G　　　　　　　　　　**F**

I've seen all _ good peo - ple turn _ their heads _

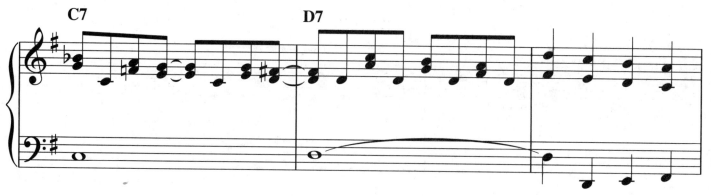

136

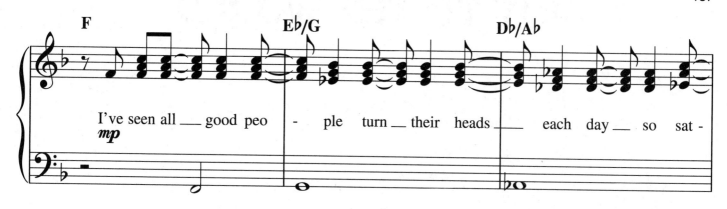

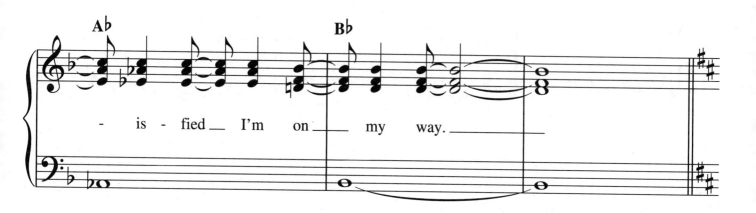

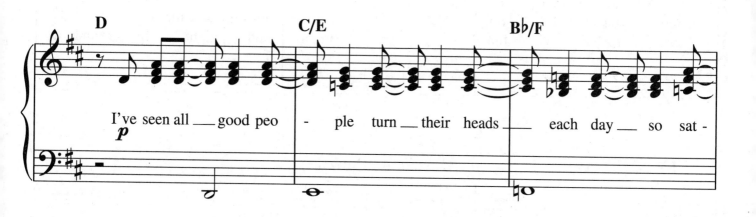

JOY TO THE WORLD

Words and Music by
HOYT AXTON

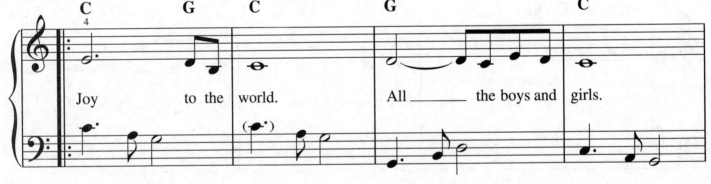

LONELY OL' NIGHT

Words and Music by
JOHN MELLENCAMP

1. She calls me up and says, "Ba - by, it's a lone-ly ol' night."
2. *(See additional lyrics)*

I don't know, _ I'm just so

scared and lone-ly all at ___ the same time. _

No-bod-y told us it was gon-na work out ___ this way, ___ no no

no no no. ___ I guess they knew we'd work ___ it out in our own way. ___

Chorus

It's a lone-ly ol'

night. ___ Can I put my arms a-round you? ___

Eb   Bb   F   Bb/F

It's a lone-ly ol' night, _____ cus-tom-made for two _

F   Fsus

_____ lone-ly peo-ple like me and you.   Yeah, like

F   Fsus   F

me and you.

Additional Lyrics

2. Radio playin' softly some singer's sad, sad song.
   He's singin' about standin' in the shadows of love.
   I guess he feels awf'lly alone.
   She says, "I know exactly what he means, yeah yeah yeah yeah yeah."
   And it's a sad, sad feelin' when you're livin' on those in-betweens,
   But it's okay.
   Chorus

JUMP

Words and Music by EDWARD VAN HALEN,
ALEX VAN HALEN and DAVID LEE ROTH

I get up

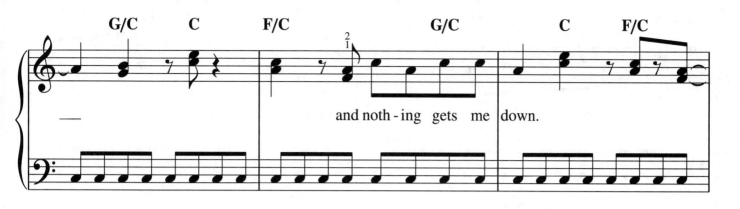

and noth-ing gets me down.

You got it tough.

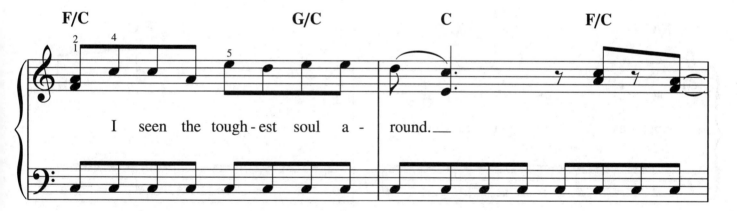

I seen the tough-est soul a - round.___

And I know, know,

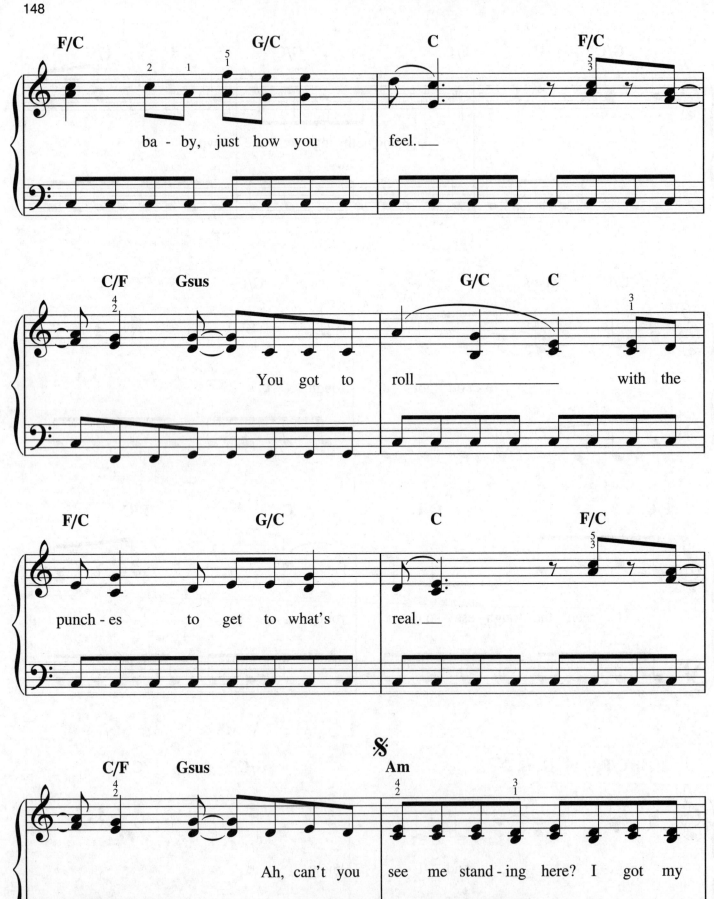

JUST WHAT I NEEDED

Words and Music by
RIC OCASEK

LAY DOWN SALLY

Words and Music by ERIC CLAPTON,
MARCY LEVY and GEORGE TERRY

Bright beat

There is noth - ing that is wrong in
sun ain't near - ly on the rise, and
long to see ____ the morn - ing rise light

want - ing you ____ to stay here ____ with me.
we still got ____ the moon and stars ____ a - bove.
col - or - ing ____ your face so dream - i - ly.

I know you've got ____ some - thing
So don't you go ____ and
Un - der - neath the

where to go, but won't you make ____ your -
vel - vet skies, love is all ____ that
say good - bye; love can lay ____ your

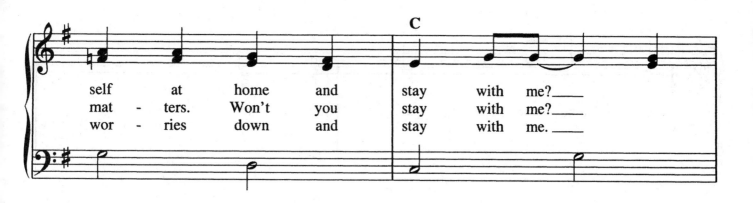

C

self at home and stay with me? ____
mat - ters. Won't you stay with me? ____
wor - ries down and stay with me. ____

D

And don't you ev - er leave. _
And don't you ev - er leave. _
And don't you ev - er leave. _

3

G

Lay down, Sal - ly, and

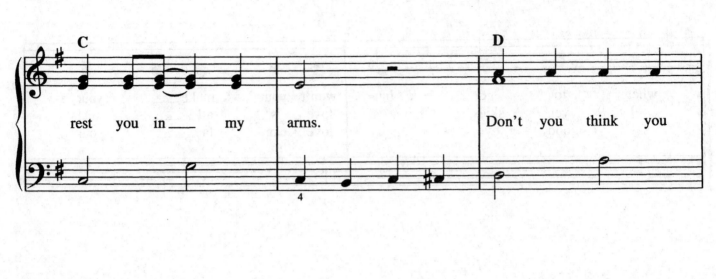

rest you in___ my arms.   Don't you think you

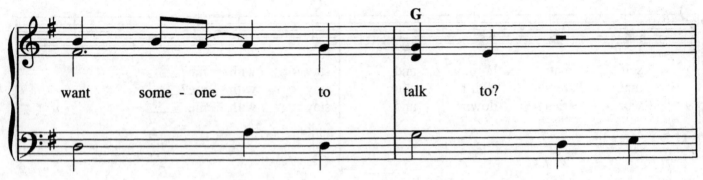

want some-one___ to   talk to?

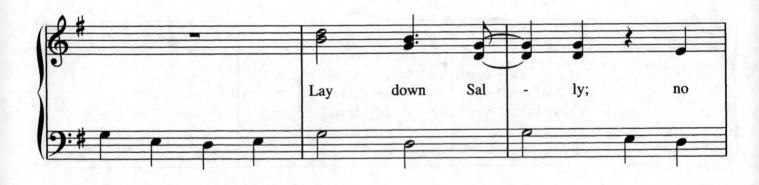

Lay down Sal - ly;   no

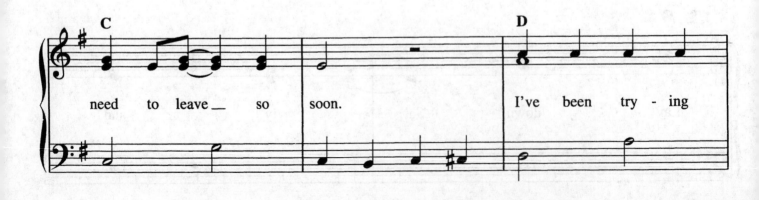

need to leave___ so soon.   I've been try - ing

LIGHTS

Words and Music by NEAL SCHON
and STEVE PERRY

When the (1., 3.) lights _____ go
(2.) think _____

down _____ in the cit - y _____ and the
you're lone - ly, _____ well, my

163

LIVIN' ON A PRAYER

Words and Music by JON BON JOVI,
DESMOND CHILD and RICHIE SAMBORA

Tom-my used to work on the docks,
Tom-my's got his six-string in hock,

un-ion's been on strike. He's down on his luck, it's tough, —
now he's hold-ing in he used to make it talk. So tough, —

so tough.
it's tough.

Gi-na works the din - er all day, — work-ing for her man. She
Gi-na dreams of run-ning a - way; — when she cries in the night, Tom-my

THE LOGICAL SONG

Words and Music by RICK DAVIES
and ROGER HODGSON

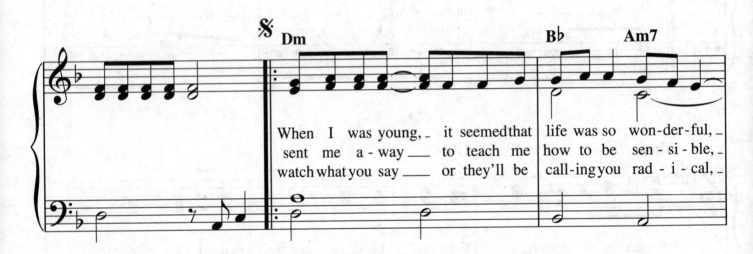

When I was young, _ it seemed that life was so won-der-ful, _
sent me a-way _ to teach me how to be sen-si-ble, _
watch what you say _ or they'll be call-ing you rad-i-cal, _

a mir-a-cle, oh, it was beau-ti-ful, mag-i-cal. And all the
log-i-cal, oh, _ re-spon-si-ble, prac-ti-cal. And then they
a lib-er-al, oh, _ fa-nat-i-cal, crim-i-nal. Oh, won't you

LOVE HURTS

Words and Music by
BOUDLEAUX BRYANT

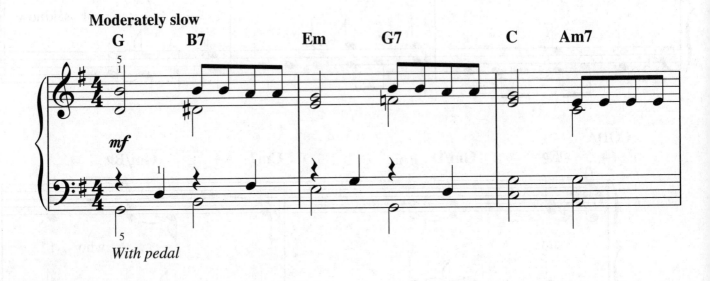

8vb

LOVE IS ALIVE

Words and Music by
GARY WRIGHT

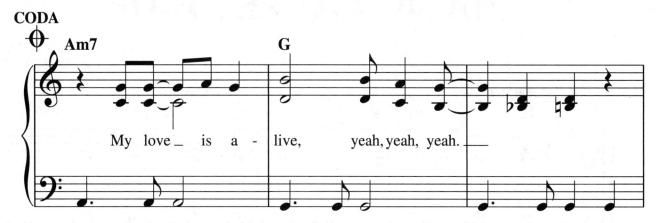

Additional Lyrics

2. Well, there's something inside
   That's making me crazy.
   I try and keep it together 'cause
   What I say may not happen the same way.
   Now could be forever and ever.
   Chorus

3. There's a mirror movin' inside my mind,
   Reflectin' the love that you shine on me.
   Hold on to the feelin'.
   Let it grow. Let it grow. Oh, yeah.
   Chorus

MAGIC CARPET RIDE

Words and Music by JOHN KAY
and RUSHTON MOREVE

MAYBE I'M AMAZED

Words and Music by
PAUL McCARTNEY

NO MATTER WHAT

Words and Music by
PETER HAM

PARADISE BY THE DASHBOARD LIGHT

Words and Music by
JIM STEINMAN

198

Ba - by, ba - by, let me sleep on it. ___ Let me

sleep on it. ___ I'll give you an an - swer in the morn -

ing. *Girl:* I got - ta

know right now! Do you love me? Will you love me for - ev - er? Do you

So now I'm pray-ing for the end of time

to hur - ry up and ar - rive. 'Cause

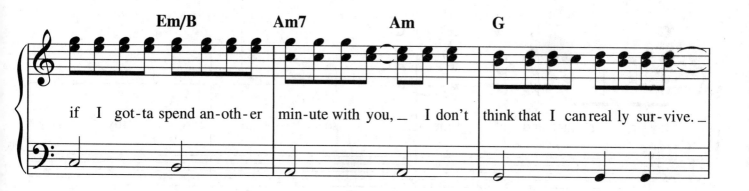

if I got-ta spend an-oth-er min-ute with you, I don't think that I can real ly sur-vive.

I'll nev - er break my prom - ise or for- get my vow, but

God on - ly knows _ what I can do right now. I'm pray-ing for the end of time, _

_ it's all that I can do. _ (Do, _ do, do.) _

Pray-ing for the end of time, _ so I can end my

time with _ you.

PEACEFUL EASY FEELING

Words and Music by
JACK TEMPCHIN

Moderately fast

mf

With pedal

I like the way _
I found out _

_ your spar - klin'
_ a long

ear - rings _
time a -

lay
go

a - gainst your
what a wom - an can

skin _ so
do to _ your

brown. _
soul. _

And I wan - na
Ah, but she

sleep with you _ in the
can't _ take _ you

know _____ you _____ as a lov-

-er and __ a friend, _____

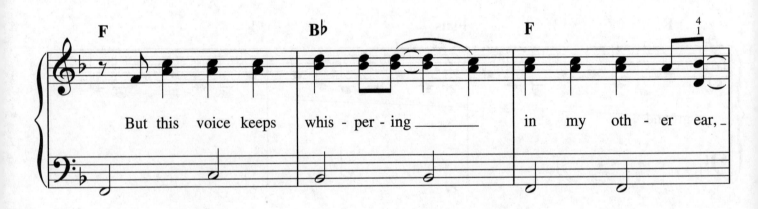

But this voice keeps whis - per - ing _____ in my oth - er ear, __

___ tells me I may nev - er see you a -

PROUD MARY

Words and Music by
JOHN FOGERTY

Left a good job___ in the cit - y,___
Cleaned a lot of plates in Mem - phis,___
If you come down___ to the riv - er,___

work - in' for the man___ ev - 'ry night and day.___
pumped a lot of 'pane___ down in New Or - leans.___
bet you gon - na find___ some peo - ple who live.

211

212

1.
rollin' on the river.
2.
rollin' on the river.
B♭
G
B♭
G
B♭
G
F
E♭
C
E♭
C
D.S. al Coda
CODA
rollin' on the river.

ROCK'N ME

Words and Music by
STEVE MILLER

___ su-per-sti - tious and I don't get sus-pi - cious, but my
Phoe-nix, Ar - i - zo - na, all the way to Ta-co - ma, Phil-a -
Phoe-nix, Ar - i - zo - na, all the way to Ta-co - ma, Phil-a -

F   **C**

wom-an is a friend of mine. ___ And I know ___ that it's true ___ that all the
del-phi - a, At-lan - ta, L. A. ___ North - ern Cal - i - for nia where the
del-phi - a, At-lan - ta, L. A. ___ North - ern Cal - i - for nia where the

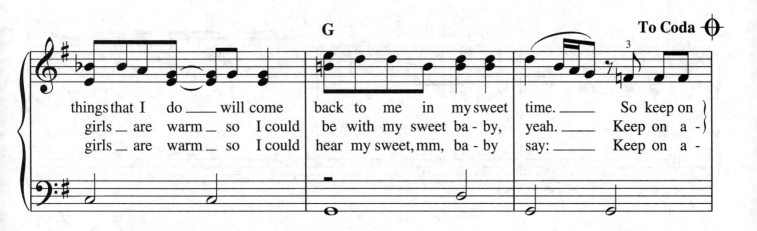

G   **To Coda ⊕**

things that I do ___ will come back to me in my sweet time. ___ So keep on
girls ___ are warm ___ so I could be with my sweet ba - by, yeah. ___ Keep on a -
girls ___ are warm ___ so I could hear my sweet, mm, ba - by say: ___ Keep on a -

F

rock-in' me, ba - by.   Keep on a - rock-in' me, ba - by.

ROCKET MAN
(I Think It's Gonna Be a Long Long Time)

Words and Music by ELTON JOHN
and BERNIE TAUPIN

Moderately slow, in 2

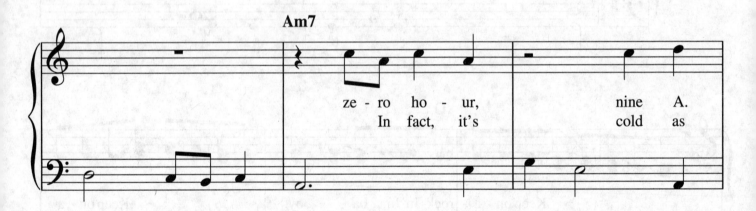

burn-ing out his fuse up here a - lone.

1. And I think it's gon-na be a long, long time.

(D.C.)

2. And I

And I think it's gon-na be a long, long time.

ROXANNE

Music and Lyrics by
STING

Moderately fast

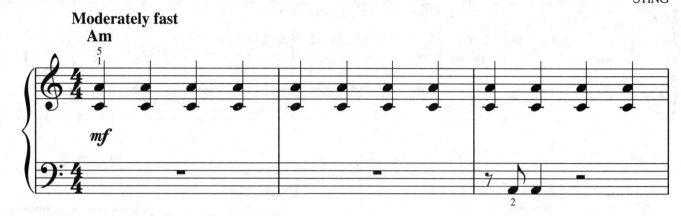

Rox - anne,
loved you since I knew ya.
you __ don't have to __ I

224

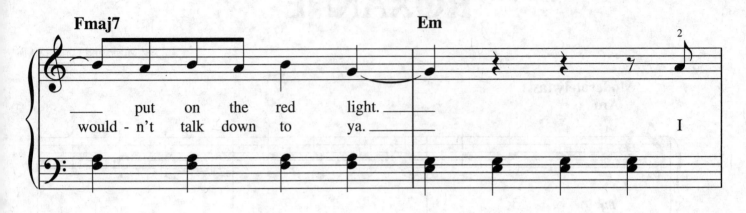

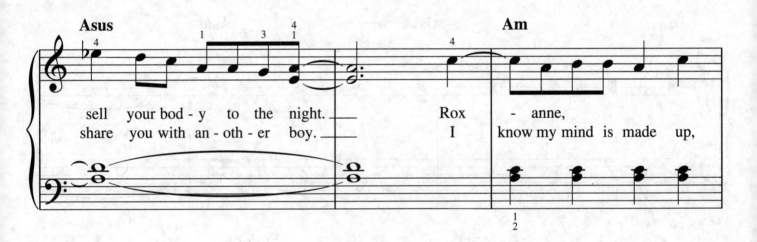

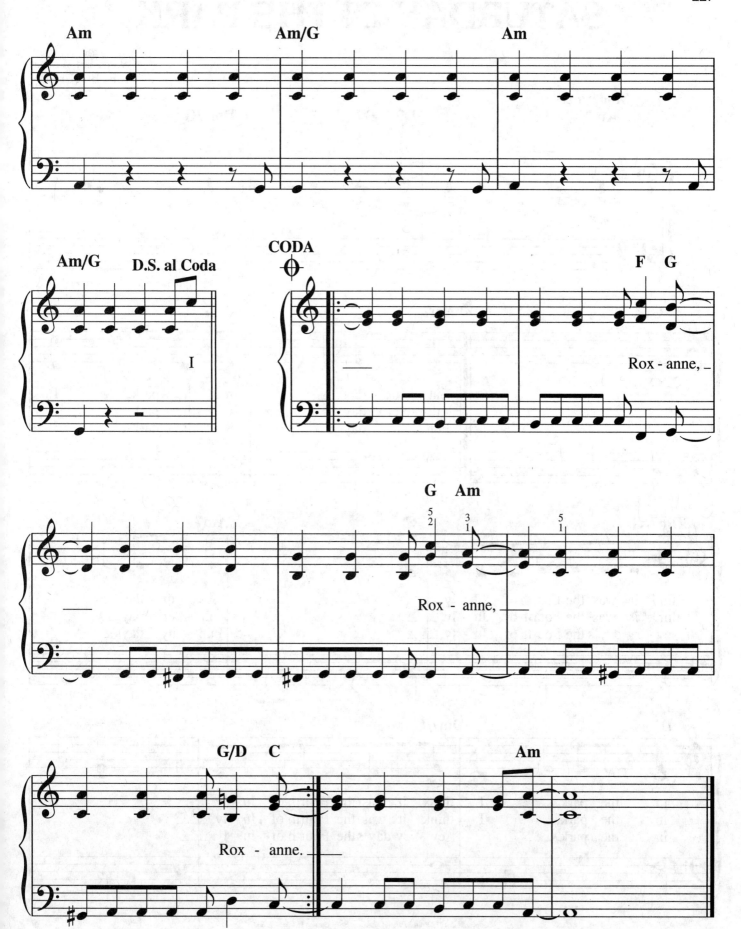

SATURDAY IN THE PARK

Words and Music by
ROBERT LAMM

230

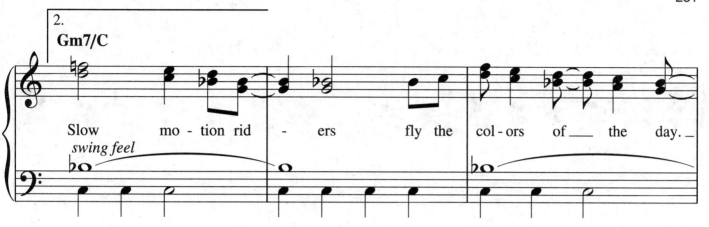

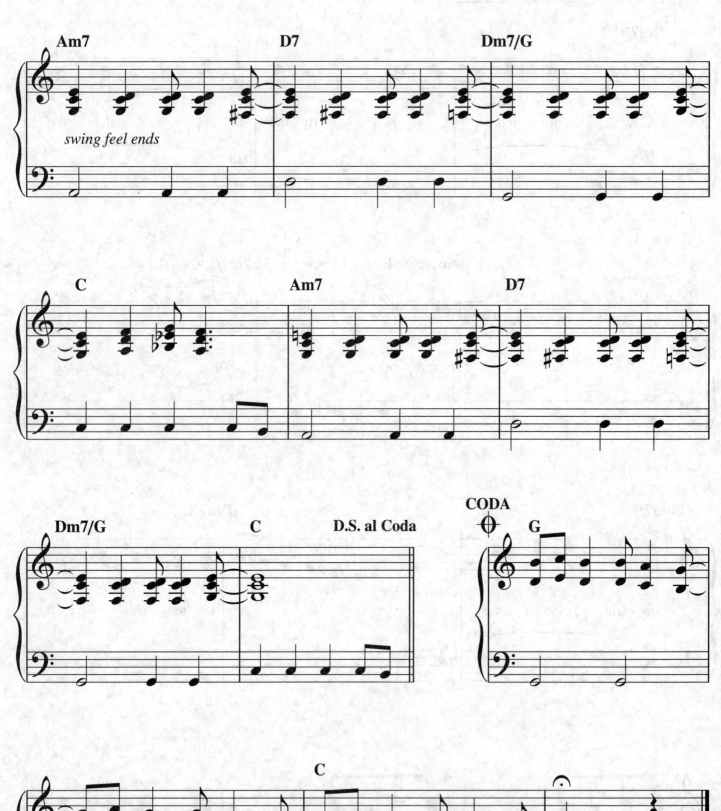

(She's)
SOME KIND OF WONDERFUL

Words and Music by
JOHN ELLISON

Moderate Rock Shuffle

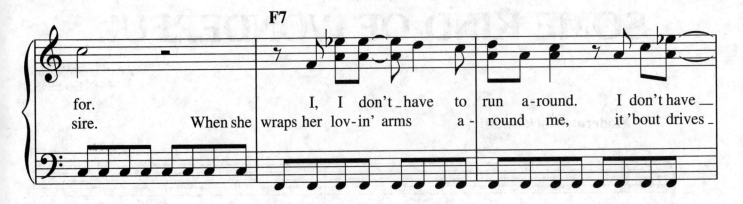

for.
sire.

I, I don't have to run a-round. I don't have
When she wraps her lov-in' arms a - round me, it 'bout drives

___ to stay out all night. 'Cause I got me a sweet, a sweet lov-in'
___ me out of my mind. Yeah, when my ba-by

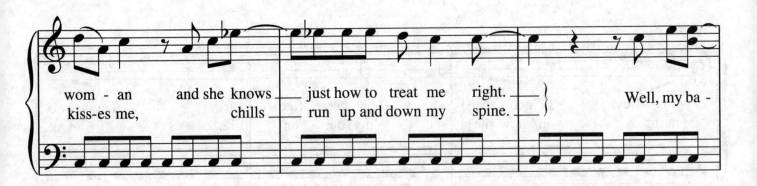

wom - an and she knows ___ just how to treat me right. ___ Well, my ba-
kiss-es me, chills ___ run up and down my spine. ___

- by, she's al - right. Well, my ba - by, she's clean out of

got a sweet lit-tle wom-an like mine? There's got to be some

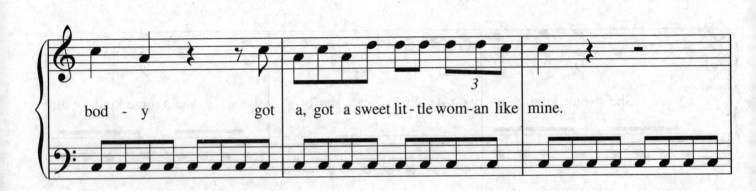

bod - y got a, got a sweet lit-tle wom-an like mine.

Now, can I get a wit - ness? Can I get a

wit - ness? Well, can I get a wit - ness?

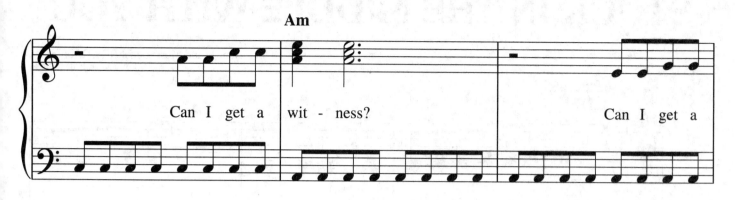

STUCK IN THE MIDDLE WITH YOU

Words and Music by GERRY RAFFERTY
and JOE EGAN

241

Yes, I'm stuck in the mid-dle with you.

Stuck in the mid-dle with you. Here I am,

stuck in the mid-dle with you.

Additional Lyrics

2. Yes, I'm stuck in the middle with you
   And I'm wond'ring what it is I should do.
   It's so hard to keep this smile on my face.
   Losing control, I'm all over the place.
   Clowns to the left of me, jokers to the right.
   Here I am, stuck in the middle with you.

3. Tryin' to make some sense of it all,
   But I can see it makes no sense at all.
   Is it cool to go to sleep on the floor?
   'Cause I don't think that I can take any more.
   Clowns to the left of me, jokers to the right.
   Here I am, stuck in the middle with you.

SUNSHINE OF YOUR LOVE

Words and Music by JACK BROWN,
PETE BROWN and ERIC CLAPTON

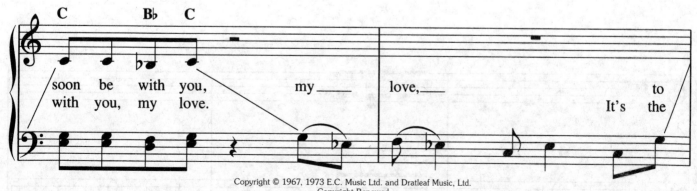

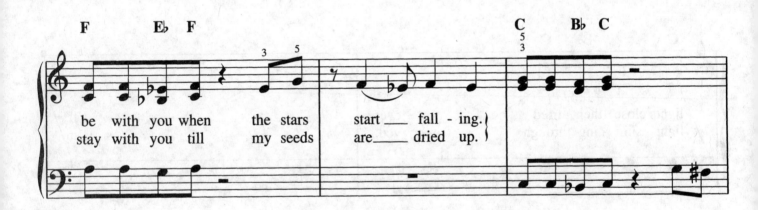

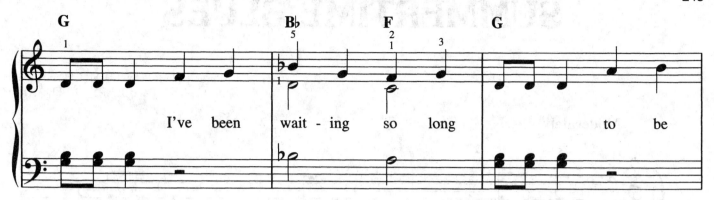

I've been wait - ing so long to be

where I'm go - ing in the sun - shine of your

love.

I'm love.

SUMMERTIME BLUES

Words and Music by EDDIE COCHRAN
and JERRY CAPEHART

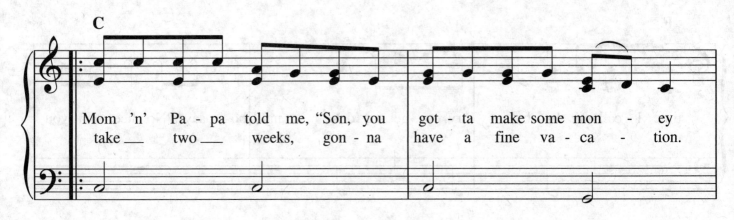

C

Mom 'n' Pa - pa told me, "Son, you got - ta make some mon - ey
take __ two __ weeks, gon - na have a fine va - ca - tion.

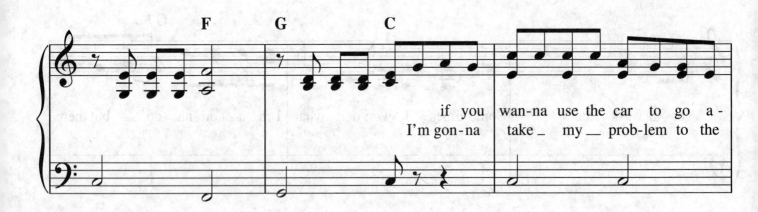

F **G** **C**

if you wan-na use the car to go a -
I'm gon-na take _ my _ prob-lem to the

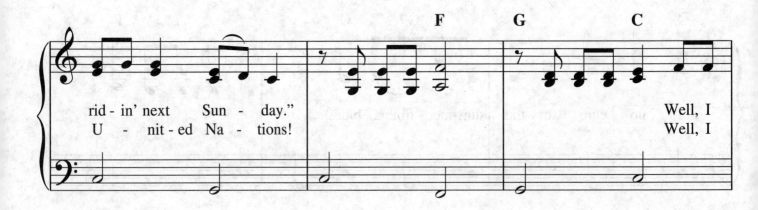

F **G** **C**

rid - in' next Sun - day."
U - nit - ed Na - tions!
Well, I
Well, I

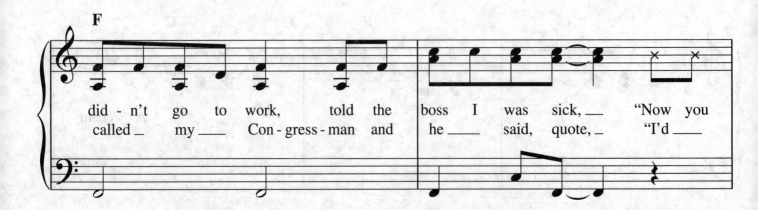

F

did - n't go to work, told the boss I was sick, __ "Now you
called _ my __ Con - gress - man and he __ said, quote, _ "I'd __

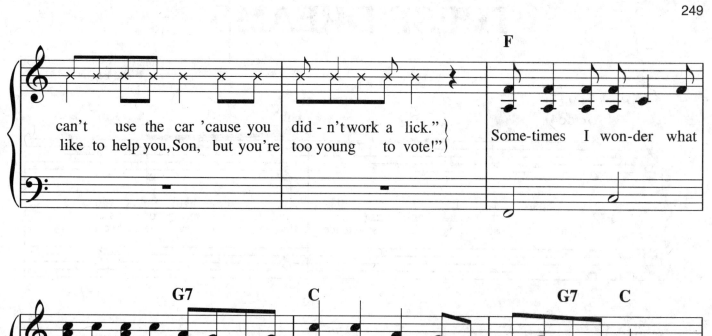

can't use the car 'cause you did-n't work a lick."
like to help you, Son, but you're too young to vote!"

F — Some-times I won-der what

G7   C   G7   C

I'm a-gon-na do, __ but there ain't no cure for the sum-mer-time _ blues.

1.   F   G   C   2.   F

I'm gon-na

G7   C   F   G   C

THESE DREAMS

Words and Music by MARTIN GEORGE PAGE
and BERNIE TAUPIN

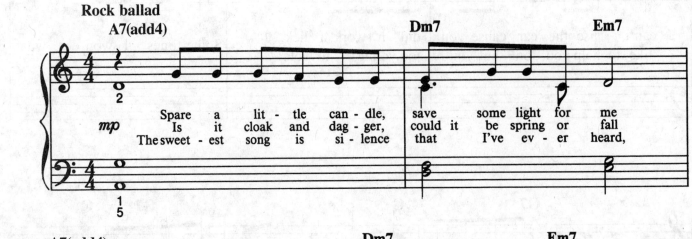

Rock ballad

A7(add4) ... Dm7 ... Em7

Spare a lit- tle can- dle, save some light for me
Is it cloak and dag- ger, could it be spring or fall
The sweet- est song is si- lence that I've ev- er heard,

A7(add4) ... Dm7 ... Em7

Fig- ures up a- head mov- ing in the trees. white
I walk with- out a cut through a stained glass wall.
Fun- ny how your feet in dreams never touch the earth. In a

Fadd9 ... Am7

skin in lin- en. Per- fume on my wrist and a
Weak- er in my eye- sight, Can- dle in my grip and
wood full of princ- es Free- dom is a kiss but the

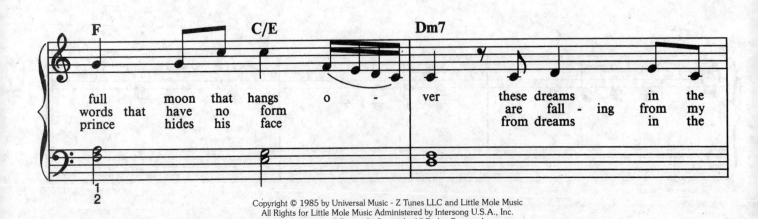

F ... C/E ... Dm7

full moon that hangs o- ver these dreams in the
words that have no form are fall- ing from my
prince hides his face from dreams in the

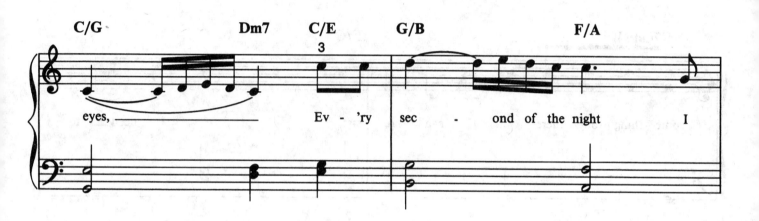

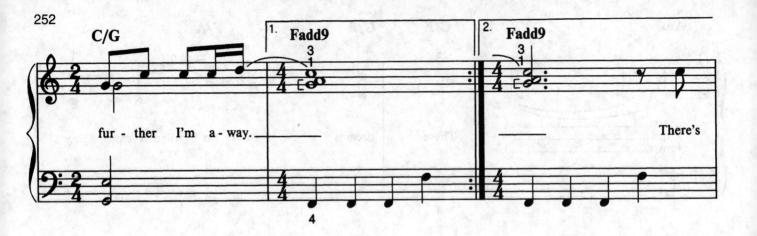

fur - ther I'm a - way. _____ _____ There's

some - thing out there I can't re - sist, I need _ to

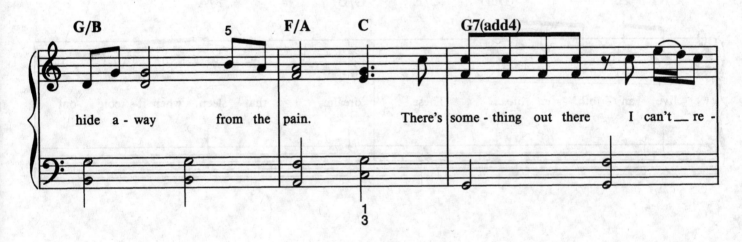

hide a - way from the pain. There's some - thing out there I can't _ re -

sist...

D.C. al Coda

fur - ther I'm a - way. _ These

dreams   go   on   when I close   my   eyes, _____ ev - 'ry

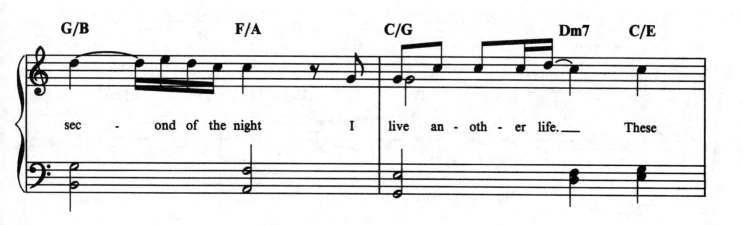

sec -   ond of the night   I   live an - oth - er life.__ These

dreams   that   sleep   when it's cold   out - side, _____ ev - 'ry

Repeat and Fade

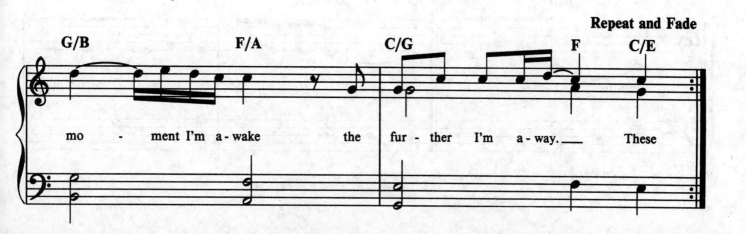

mo -   ment I'm a - wake   the   fur - ther I'm a - way.__ These

TIME

Words and Music by DARIUS CARLOS RUCKER,
EVERETT DEAN FELBER, MARK WILLIAM BRYAN
and JAMES GEORGE SONEFELD

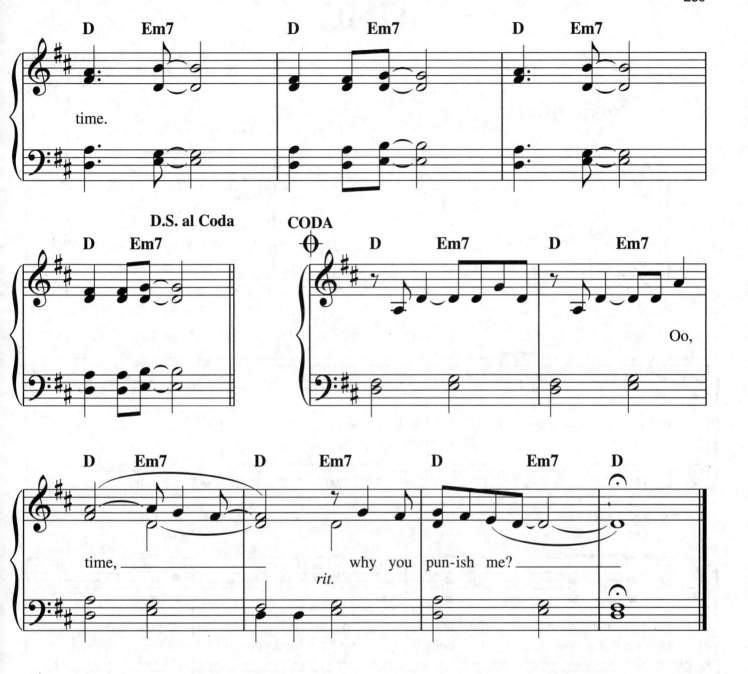

Additional Lyrics

2. Time, take their red and blue.
   Wash them in the ocean, make them clean.
   Maybe their mothers won't cry tonight.

3. Time, you left me standin' there,
   Like a tree growin' all alone.
   The wind just stripped me bare, stripped me bare.

4. Time, the past has come and gone.
   The future's far away.
   Well, now only lasts for one second, one second.

TIME

Words and Music by ROGER WATERS,
NICHOLAS MASON, DAVID GILMOUR
and RICK WRIGHT

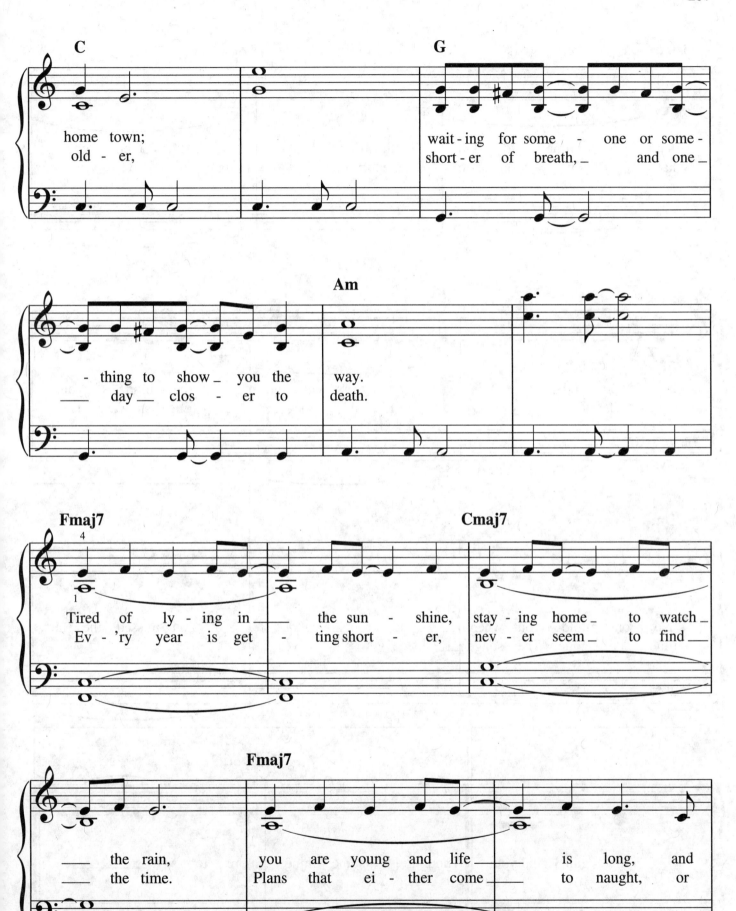

WALK OF LIFE

Words and Music by
MARK KNOPFLER

1. Here comes John - ny sing - ing old - ies, gold - ies,
2. Here comes John - ny and he'll tell you a sto - ry.

be - bop - a - lu - la ba - by what I say. ___ Here comes John - ny sing - ing
Hand me down my walk - in' shoes, ___ Here comes John - ny with the

I got a wom - an down in the tun - nels trying to make it pay.
pow'r and the glo - ry, back beat the talk - in' blues.

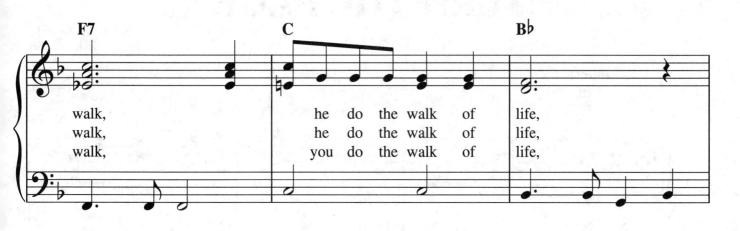

walk,
walk,
walk,

he do the walk of life,
he do the walk of life,
you do the walk of life,

yeah, he do the walk of life.
yeah, he do the walk of life.
mm, you do the walk of life.

To Coda ⊕

1.

2. D.S. al Coda
(Verse 1)

CODA

TURN THE PAGE

Words and Music by
BOB SEGER

1. On a long and lone-some high-way____
2., 3. *(See additional lyrics)*

east of O - ma-ha you can lis-ten to the en-gine moan-in'

out its one___ note song, you can think a-bout___ the wom-an or the

Say, here I am on the

road a-gain.___ There I am up on the stage.___ Here I

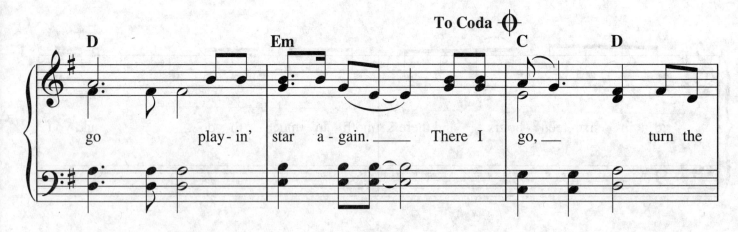

go playin' star a-gain.___ There I go,___ turn the

page.

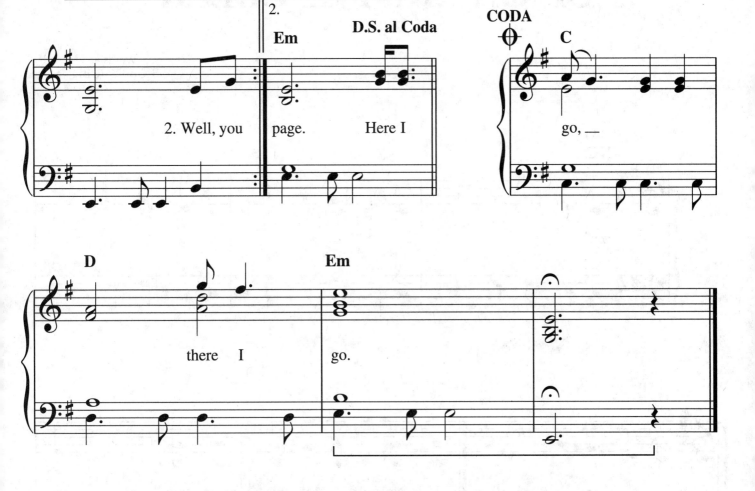

Additional Lyrics

2. Well, you walk into a restaurant strung out from the road
   And you feel the eyes upon you as you're shakin' off the cold;
   You pretend it doesn't bother you, but you just want to explode.
   Most times you can't hear 'em talk, other times you can,
   All the same old cliches, "Is that a woman or a man?"
   And you always seem out numbered, you don't dare make a stand.
   Chorus

3. Out there in the spotlight, you're a million miles away.
   Every ounce of energy you try to give away
   As the sweat pours out your body like the music that you play.
   Later in the evening, you lie awake in bed
   With the echoes from the amplifiers ringing in your head.
   You smoke the day's last cigarette remembering what she said.
   Chorus

UP ON CRIPPLE CREEK

Words and Music by
ROBBIE ROBERTSON

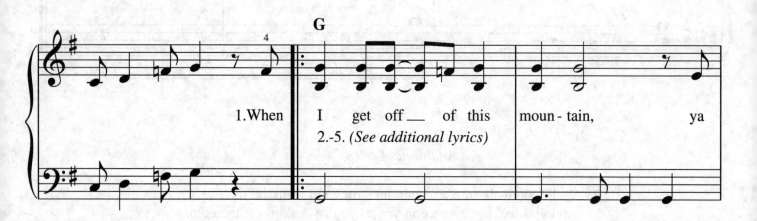

1.When I get off __ of this moun-tain, ya
2.-5. *(See additional lyrics)*

know where I wan-na go? ____

Straight down _ the Mis-

C **D** **D7**

-sis-sip-pi Riv-er to the Gulf of Mex - i - co. To

G **C**

Lake Charles, Lou - 'si - an - na, Lit - tle Bes - sie, girl I once

G **Cmaj7**

knew ___ And she told ___ me just to come on by, ___ If there's

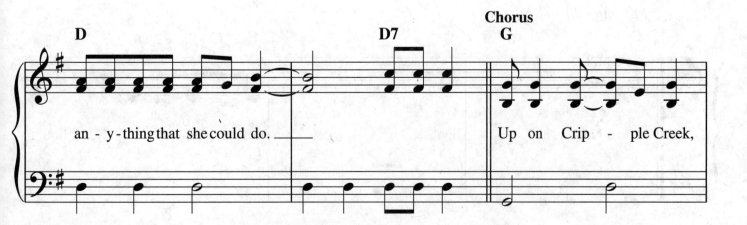

D **D7** **Chorus** **G**

an - y-thing that she could do. ___ Up on Crip - ple Creek,

272

she sends me; If I spring a leak, she mends me;

I don't have to speak 'cause she de-fends me. A drunk-ard's dream if I

ev - er did see one.

Play after 4th and 5th verses.

No, no, hoo. Lo - dy, lo - dy, lo - dy, hoo.

Additional Lyrics

2. Good luck had just stung me, to the race track I did go.
   She bet on one horse to win and I bet on another to show.
   The odds were in my favor, I had 'em five to one,
   When that nag to win came around the track, sure enough she had won.
   Chorus

3. I took up all my winnings, and I gave my little Bessie half.
   She tore it up and threw it in my face, just for a laugh.
   Now there's one thing in the whole wide world, I sure would like to see:
   That's when that little love of mine dips her doughnut in my tea.
   Chorus

4. Now me and my mate were back at the shack, we had Spike Jones on the box.
   She said, "I can't take the way he sings, but I love to hear him talk."
   Now that just gave my heart a throb, to the bottom of my feet,
   And I swore as I took another pull, my Bessie can't be beat.
   Chorus

5. Now there's a flood out in California, and up north it's freezing cold,
   And this living on the road is getting pretty old.
   So I guess I'll call my big mamma, tell her I'll be rolling in.
   But you know, deep down, I'm kind of tempted to go and see my Bessie again.
   Chorus

WALK ON THE WILD SIDE

Words and Music by
LOU REED

Moderately

1. Hol-ly came from Mi-am-i F - L - A,   hitch-hiked her way a-cross the U. S.

2.-5. *(See additional lyrics)*

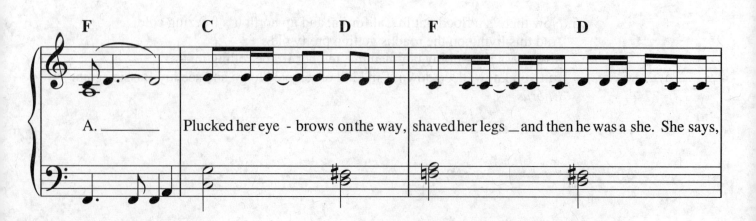

A. _____   Plucked her eye - brows on the way,   shaved her legs _ and then he was a she. She says,

doo doo doo doo doo doo doo doo. (Doo doo doo doo doo doo doo doo doo doo doo doo doo doo doo doo doo doo

doo doo doo doo doo doo doo doo doo doo doo doo doo doo doo doo.)

To Coda ⊕

D.S. al Coda
(with repeats)

CODA ⊕

rit.

Additional Lyrics

2. Candy came from out on the island.
   In the back room she was ev'rybody's darling.
   But she never lost her head even when she was givin' head. She says,
   "Hey, babe, take a walk on the wild side,
   Said hey, Joe, take a walk on the wild side."

3. Little Joe never once gave it away,
   Ev'rybody had to pay and pay.
   Hustle here and hustle there, New York City is the place, where they said:
   "Hey, babe, take a walk on the wild side,
   Said hey, babe, take a walk on the wild side."

4. Sugar Plum Fairy came and hit the streets
   lookin' for soul food and a place to eat.
   Went to the Apollo, you shoulda seen 'em go, go, go. They said,
   "Hey, sugar, take a walk on the wild side,
   Said hey, babe, take a walk on the wild side."

5. Jackie is just speedin' away.
   Thought she was James Dean for a day.
   Then, I guess, she had to crash. Valium would have helped that bash. She said,
   "Hey, babe, take a walk on the wild side,
   Said hey, honey, take a walk on the wild side."

WE ARE THE CHAMPIONS

Words and Music by
FREDDIE MERCURY

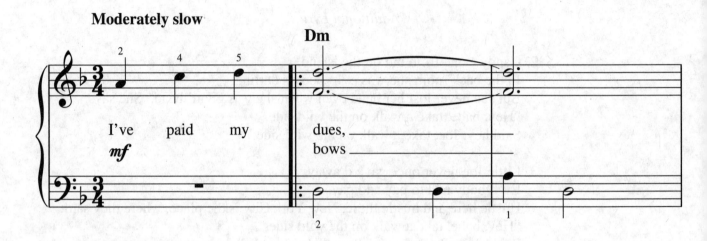

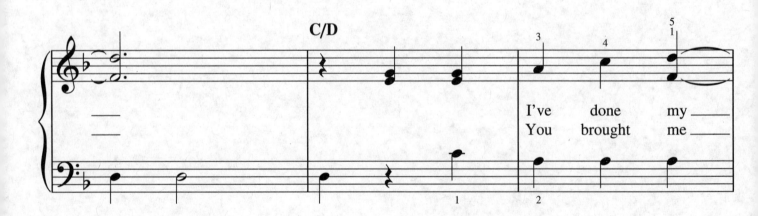

I've had my | share of | sand___ | kicked in___ my___
sid - er it a | chal - lenge | be - fore | the whole_ hu - man

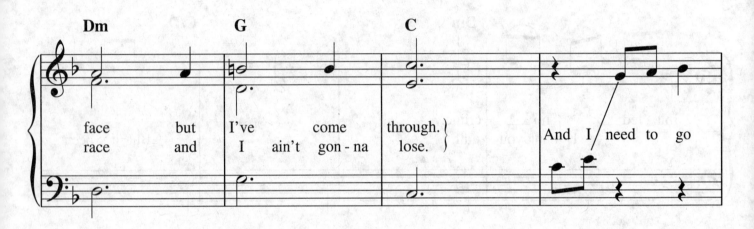

face | but | I've come | through. } | And I need to go
race | and | I ain't gon - na | lose. }

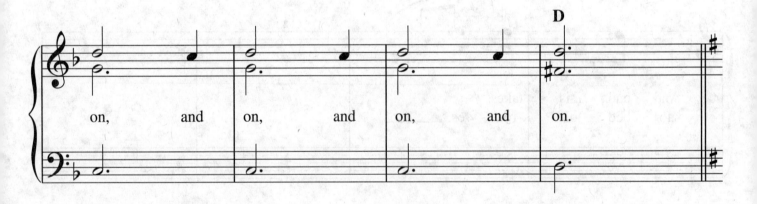

on, | and | on, | and | on, | and | on.

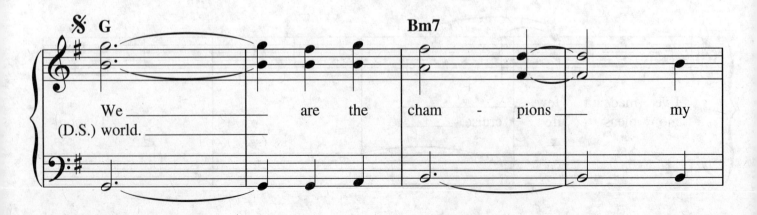

We___ | are the cham - pions___ my
(D.S.) world. ___

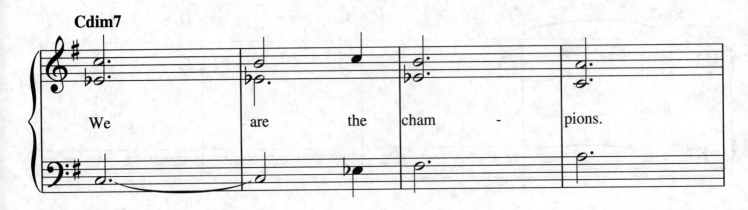

Cdim7

We   are   the   cham -   pions.

G   **Am7**

No   time   for   los -   ers,   'cause

To Coda ⊕ **C7**

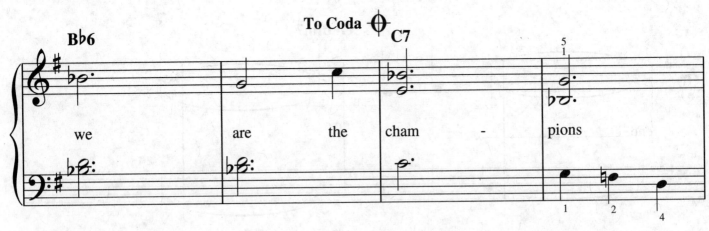

Bb6

we   are   the   cham -   pions

1.

D7sus   **Gm**

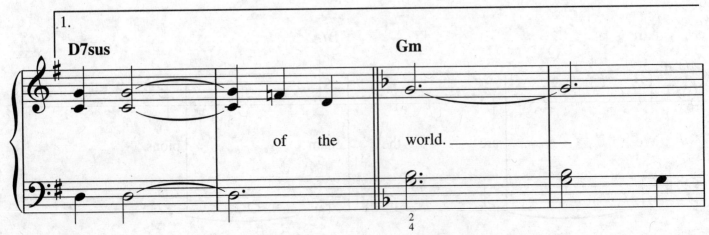

of   the   world.

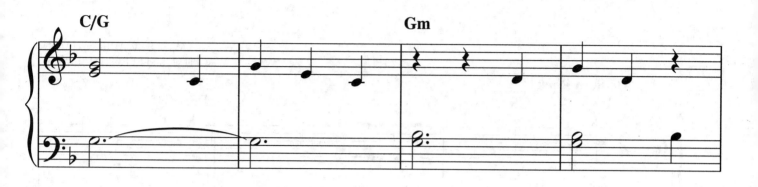

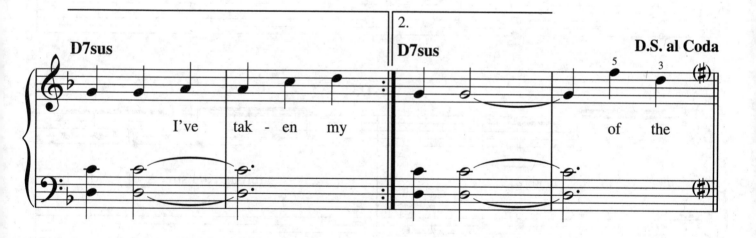

I've tak - en my

of the

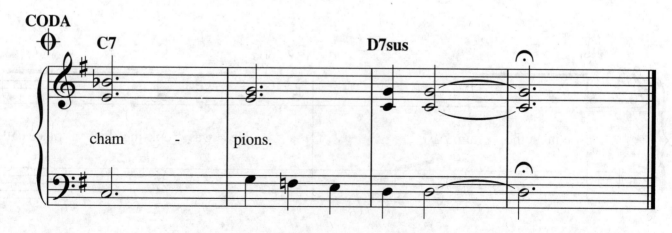

CODA

cham - pions.

WEREWOLVES OF LONDON

Words and Music by WARREN ZEVON,
WADDY WACHTEL and LEROY MARINELL

I saw a were-wolf with a Chi-nese
(See additional lyrics)

men-u in his hand, _____

walk-ing through the streets of So-ho_

_____ in the rain. _____

He was look-ing for a place called

Additional Lyrics

He's the hairy-handed gent who ran amuck in Kent;
Lately, he's been overheard in Mayfair.
You better stay away from him!
He'll rip your lungs out, Jim!
Huh! I'd like to meet his tailor.

Ow-oo! Werewolves of London.
Ow-oo!
Ow-oo! Werewolves of London.
Ow-oo!

Well, I saw Lon Chaney walking with the Queen,
Doin' the werewolves of London.
I saw Lon Chaney Junior walking with the Queen,
Doin' the werewolves of London.

WILD NIGHT

Words and Music by
VAN MORRISON

A WHITER SHADE OF PALE

Words and Music by KEITH REID,
GARY BROOKER and MATTHEW FISHER

1. We skipped the light fan-
2. She said, "I'm home on
3. *(See additional lyrics)*

dan - go, _____   turned cart-wheels 'cross the
shore leave," _____   though in truth we were at

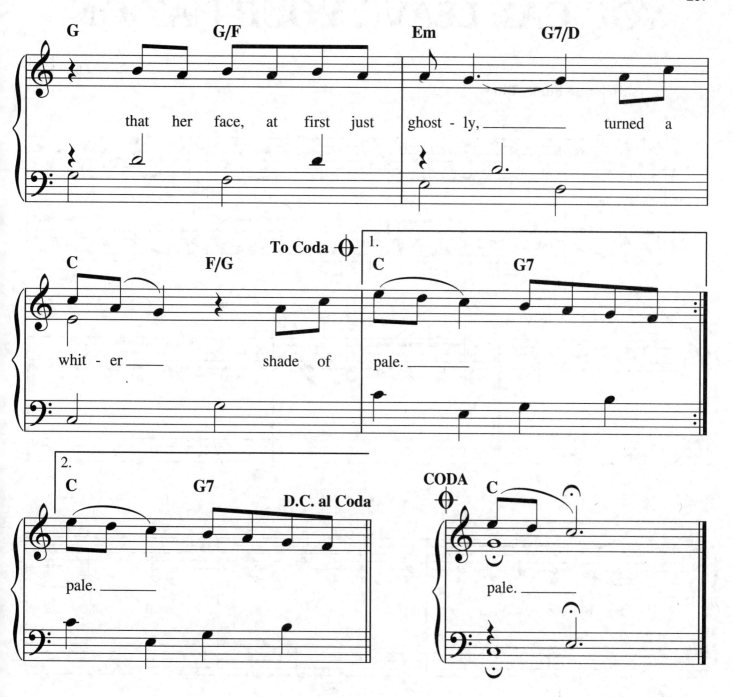

Additional Lyrics

3. She said, "There is no reason,
   And the truth is plain to see."
   But I wandered through my playing cards
   And would not let her be
   One of sixteen vestal virgins
   Who were leaving for the coast.
   And although my eyes were open,
   They might just as well been closed.

YOU CAN LEAVE YOUR HAT ON

Words and Music by
RANDY NEWMAN

Moderate Funky Blues

Hal Leonard Piano White Pages

Modeled after our best-selling *Guitar Tab White Pages*, these books could be the best piano compilations ever!

Piano White Pages

200 songs, including: Amazed • Brown Eyed Girl • California Dreamin' • Clocks • Come Sail Away • Come to My Window • Dancing Queen • Do You Really Want to Hurt Me • Dust in the Wind • Easy • Fast Car • Free Bird • Good Vibrations • Happy Together • Hot Hot Hot • I Hope You Dance • I Will Remember You • I Will Survive • Jack and Diane • Landslide • Oops!...I Did It Again • Smooth • Tears in Heaven • These Boots Are Made for Walkin' • Time After Time • Walking in Memphis • Werewolves of London • You Can't Hurry Love • You've Got a Friend • You've Lost That Lovin' Feelin' • and many more.
00311276 P/V/G $29.99

Piano White Pages Volume 2

200 more songs, with no duplication from Volume 1! This volume includes: All by Myself • Annie's Song • At Seventeen • Autumn Leaves • Beyond the Sea • Blowin' in the Wind • Bridge over Troubled Water • Candle in the Wind • Don't Know Why • Don't Stop Believin' • Downtown • Hello Again • Hey Jude • I Will Always Love You • I Write the Songs • Longer • Lullaby of Birdland • Misty • Mona Lisa • Morning Has Broken • My Funny Valentine • My Way • Puttin' on the Ritz • The Rainbow Connection • Rumour Has It • Satin Doll • Someone like You • Time After Time • Up Where We Belong • We've Only Just Begun • Woman • You Are So Beautiful • You're the Inspiration • and more.
00312562 P/V/G $29.99

Prices, contents and availability subject to change without notice.

7777 W. BLUEMOUND RD. P.O. BOX 13819 MILWAUKEE, WI 53213

www.halleonard.com

Broadway Piano White Pages

The ultimate collection of every Broadway song you'll ever need – over 200 in all – arranged for piano and voice with guitar chord frames. This amazing folio features: All the Things You Are • And All That Jazz • Another Suitcase in Another Hall • Any Dream Will Do • Big Spender • Bring Him Home • Brotherhood of Man • Consider Yourself • Dancing on the Ceiling • Give My Regards to Broadway • I Am Changing • I Could Have Danced All Night • I Don't Know How to Love Him • On My Own • One • Seasons of Love • The Sound of Music • A Spoonful of Sugar • Tomorrow • We Go Together • and more. 896 pages!
00311500 P/V/G $29.99

Easy Piano White Pages

The largest collection of easy piano arrangements ever, with 200 songs and over 860 pages! Includes: Alison • Bennie and the Jets • Bridge over Troubled Water • California Girls • Crazy Little Thing Called Love • Don't Worry, Be Happy • Footloose • Hey, Soul Sister • I Get Around • If I Were a Carpenter • King of the Road • Layla • Maybe I'm Amazed • My Girl • Night Moves • Peter Gunn • Saving All My Love for You • Take Me Home, Country Roads • Walk This Way • You Are My Sunshine • and many, many more!
00312566 Easy Piano $29.99

The E-Z Play® Today White Pages

More than 330 hits in all styles fill 900 pages in the largest collection ever of songs in our world-famous notation! Features: All of Me • Big Spender • Brian's Song • Color My World • Come Fly with Me • Dancing Queen • Dream Weaver • Fly like an Eagle • The Godfather Theme • Guilty • Jackson • Lush Life • Monday, Monday • Moon River • Puppy Love • Rockin' Robin • Skylark • Tangerine • Truly • The Very Thought of You • Y.M.C.A. • You Raise Me Up • and scores more!
00100234 E-Z Play Today #316 .... $27.99